William J. W. Roome

Blessed be Egypt

a missionary story - being some account of present missionary effort in Egypt, and the story of the Lord's leading of the Egypt mission band

William J. W. Roome

Blessed be Egypt

a missionary story - being some account of present missionary effort in Egypt, and the story of the Lord's leading of the Egypt mission band

ISBN/EAN: 9783337227449

Printed in Europe, USA, Canada, Australia, Japan

Cover: Foto ©Lupo / pixelio.de

More available books at **www.hansebooks.com**

"Blessed be Egypt"

A MISSIONARY STORY

BEING

SOME ACCOUNT OF PRESENT MISSIONARY
EFFORT IN EGYPT, AND THE STORY OF THE LORD'S
LEADING OF THE EGYPT MISSION BAND

EDITED BY
WM. J. W. ROOME, M.S.A.

London:
MARSHALL BROTHERS,
KESWICK HOUSE, PATERNOSTER ROW.
1898.

CONTENTS.

	PAGE.
PREFACE	vii.
CHAPTER I.—INTRODUCTORY	11
,, II.—"THE LABOURERS"	14
,, III.—THE ORDINATION OF THE "PIERCED HANDS"	30
,, IV.—DELIVERANCE AND TRANSLATION	40
,, V.—THE LAND AND ITS PEOPLE	73
,, VI.—THE PRE-EMINENCE OF PRAYER IN CONNECTION WITH MISSIONS, AND OUR DUTY TOWARDS EGYPT.	93

How Long?

By Rev. A. B. Simpson.

There's a cry comes forth from the heavenly temple,
   'Mid the hush of the seraphim's song,
'Tis the souls of the martyrs under the altar:
   " How long, O Lord, how long?"

There's an echo falls from the heavenly temple,
   With a message so stern and so strong,
'Tis the voice of the Lord as He asks of His people:
   " How long, My Church, how long?"

There's a cry goes out from the whole creation,
   Like a burden of anguish and wrong;
'Tis the groan of the earth for the day of redemption,
   It is saying, " O Lord, how long?"

There's a bitter cry from the depths of the darkness,
   Where the perishing heathen throng;
'Tis the cry of a thousand millions pleading,
   " How long, O Lord, how long?"

They are suffering, sinning, and dying yonder,
   With no one to pity their cry;
They are passing away to a darker dying,
   How long will we let them die?

There are weeping women, wronged and helpless,
   And their life is a living pain;
There are murdered children, with none to save them,
   How long shall they weep in vain?

It is long since the love of Jesus found us,
   But no one has cared for their woe;
They have never been told of the Christ that saved you,
   O why do you not go?

Would we speed the hour of the Master's coming,
   Would we bring the eternal song,
Let us rouse from our slumber and hark to the summons:
   " How long! how long! how long!"

They are longing there for the Master's coming,
   And the meeting with loved ones again,
Can we bear to delay that glorious meeting?
   Can we let them cry in vain?

PREFACE.

IF any apology were needed for adding to the multitude of books, the events of the past few weeks in the Soudan should be sufficient call to draw the attention of all interested in the spread of the Redeemer's kingdom to the "GREAT OPPORTUNITY" that is opening for aggressive missionary effort in the immense country, now coming under the flag of a Christian nation. Another reason for issuing this small book is to shew forth the glory of our Lord and Master in calling out, and separating, and sending forth a band of Seven Young Men to that ancient land.

For the encouragement of God's children in a wider circle than that reached by the immediate friends of the brethren, we would seek to emphasize the work of the Holy Spirit in thus dealing with these brethren individually, and laying "the burden of Egypt" so heavily on the hearts of many of His children that they have been led to pray definitely for that wonderful nation.

We are confident the Lord must have wonderful purposes for the future of that people, when politically, nationally, and spiritually He is focussing such attention upon them.

About two years ago, in the city of Belfast, the Lord began to draw together a band of young men, gathered from all Evangelical denominations, for two distinct objects:—To preach the Gospel on Saturday evenings in the open air, and to meet once a week for a "Half-night of Prayer." They became knit together by the bonds of a deep spiritual longing for the perishing and love for the Master, Whom they desired to serve. The "Life Stories" in this book will reveal how the Lord led on that band, so that in the short space of about eighteen months, out of a total of thirteen, seven had received clear and distinct calls to the "Regions Beyond," one had been chosen pastor to a vacant congregation, and two others had been set apart as evangelists. We would say no word that could give praise to man, but seek to centre all glory on the Wonderful and Gracious Lord, Who so condescends to take the broken and empty vessel and use it for His own purposes of grace. This we may say, what He has done for one, He can and will do for all who "leave all and follow Him" in whole-hearted surrender and consecration. If this little effort lead some brother or sister thus to "follow the Lamb whithersoever He goeth," we will rejoice and give God the glory.

Much interest was manifested by God's people in the farewell addresses and testimonies of the first five to sail in January of this year, and many expressed the wish for some more permanent record of them. All the brethren were known in business and social circles, and their going forth proved a blessing to many.

The sincerest thanks are due to all who have kindly contributed—to Miss Van Sommer, who has known the land for many years; to the Rev. George Macgregor, M.A., who pleads for earnest prayer on behalf of the "Regions Beyond"; to Rev. George Grubb, M.A., for the prophetical outline of God's purposes; to Herr Baedeker for kindly granting permission to make use of his valuable guide to Egypt in describing the "Land and its People;" to the A.U.P.M., the C.M.S., and the N.A.M. for particulars of their Missions, which are doing so much good in the large cities of the Delta district, and the villages on the banks of the Nile; to the members of the band who have gone forth in the name of the Lord, giving their lives to Him for that land; to Mr. A. W. Vance, the *Hon. Treasurer* of the E.M.B., and Mr. J. E. Pim, the *Hon. Secretary* of the E.M.B. Prayer Circle; and to the Authors of poems, which so help the spirit of the book.

This book professes no literary merit. It has had to be compiled hurriedly, amidst the pressure of business, to be ready for the farewell meeting of the last two to sail for Egypt.

With earnest prayer that the promise, "Blessed be Egypt," may be abundantly fulfilled, and many of God's children in the homeland take a deeper interest in that ancient people, and some at least be led by His Blessed Spirit to lay their "all" on His altar, and go forth at His command; and also that the Lord's dealing with these young men may prove an encouragement to many others to look to the Holy Spirit of God alone for guidance in their daily life and supply of their every need, is this little book sent forth in the name of our Risen Saviour.

BELFAST, *Sept. 26, 1898.*   WM. J. W. ROOME.

"He Was Not Willing."

"He was not willing that any should perish;"
    Jesus, enthron'd in the glory above,
Saw our poor fallen world, pitied our sorrows,
    Pour'd out His life for us—wonderful love!
Perishing! perishing! thronging our pathway,
    Hearts break with burdens too heavy to bear,
Jesus would save, but there's no one to tell them,
    No one to lift them from sin and despair.

"He was not willing that any should perish;"
    Cloth'd in our flesh with its sorrow and pain,
Came He to seek the lost, comfort the mourner,
    Heal the heart broken by sorrow and shame.
Perishing! perishing! harvest is passing,
    Reapers are few, and the night draweth near;
Jesus is calling thee, haste to the reaping,
    Thou shalt have souls, precious souls for thy hire.

Plenty for pleasure, but little for Jesus;
    Time for the world with its troubles and toys,
No time for Jesus' work, feeding the hungry,
    Lifting lost souls to eternity's joys.
Perishing! perishing! hark, how they call us:
    "Bring us your Saviour, oh, tell us of Him!
We are so weary, so heavily-laden,
    And with long weeping, our eyes have grown dim."

"He was not willing that any should perish;"
    Am I His follower, and can I live
Longer at ease with a soul going downward,
    Lost for the lack of the help I might give?
Perishing! perishing! Thou wast not willing;
    Master, forgive, and inspire us anew;
Banish our worldliness, help us to ever
    Live with eternity's values in view.

A STREET SCENE—REFRESHMENT BY THE WAY.

"BLESSED BE EGYPT."

CHAPTER I.

Introductory.

"Whom the Lord of hosts shall bless, saying, Blessed be Egypt, My people, ..."—Isa. xix. 25.

> Armies of prayer the promise claim,
> Prove the full power of Jesus' name
>   And take the victory.
> Your conquering Captain leads you on ;
> The glorious fight may still be won
>   The coming century.

AFTER long dark centuries in the history of Egypt, a brighter day seems dawning under the rule of a Christian nation, and it is a fitting time for the prayer of faith to ascend to the most High God for Egypt and Ethiopia. The Hebrew "Cush," translated "Ethiopia," denotes rather what is known as the Soudan than Abyssinia. Many of the Lord's people in these days are seeking to be filled with the knowledge of His will in all wisdom and spiritual understanding, and thus to enter intelligently into the heart sympathies of the Son of God, Who loved them and gave Himself up for them.

The Scripture of truth tells us that He has wondrous purposes of grace towards Egypt and the Soudan. When these purposes have been fulfilled "Israel shall be the third with Egypt and with Assyria, the work of My hands, and Israel Mine inheritance." We may gather from this passage that Israel, Egypt, and Assyria are to be blessed contemporaneously. For several years past God has been dealing wondrously, both politically and spiritually, with the dry bones of Israel. His political dealings with Egypt have been no less wonderful, and as we seek to interpret these dealings by the prophetic writings, we cannot doubt that the set time to favour Egypt, the Soudan, and Asia Minor is dawning.

The 18th, 19th, and 20th chapters of Isaiah reveal to us some of the blessings in store for Egypt, Cush, and "the land beyond the rivers of Cush."

"*The burden of Egypt. Behold, the Lord rideth upon a swift cloud, and shall come into Egypt: and the idols of Egypt shall be moved at His presence, and the heart of Egypt shall melt in the midst of it. And I will set the Egyptians against the Egyptians: and they shall fight everyone against his brother, and everyone against his neighbour; city against city, and kingdom against kingdom. And the spirit of Egypt shall fail in the midst thereof; and I will destroy the counsel thereof: and they shall seek to the idols, and to the charmers, and to them that have familiar spirits, and to the wizards. And the Egyptians will I give over into the hand of a cruel lord; and a fierce king shall rule over them, saith the Lord, the Lord of Hosts.*

"*In that day shall there be an altar to the Lord in the midst of the land of Egypt, and a pillar at the border thereof to the Lord. And it shall be for a sign and for a witness unto the Lord of Hosts in the land of Egypt: for they shall cry unto the Lord because of the oppressors, and He shall send them a Saviour, and a great one, and He shall deliver them.*"—ISAIAH xix. 1, 2, 3, 4, 19, 20.

This blessing, too, seems to be brought about at a time of great political unrest, as indicated in Isaiah xvii. 12, 13 (R.V.):—

"Ah, the uproar of many peoples, which roar like the roaring of the seas; and the rushing of nations, that rush like the rushing of mighty waters! The nations shall rush like the rushing of many waters : but He shall rebuke them, and they shall flee far off, and shall be chased as the chaff of the mountains before the wind, and like the whirling dust before the storm."

Even the mutual jealousies and the "rushing" of the nations will have to work out the will of God in the whole earth.

Christian men and women, you who desire to dwell in the secret place of the Most High, and thus learn the secret of the Lord, will you not begin from this day to pour out your soul for Egypt and the Soudan? As the nations "rush" madly along, and we see the day approaching, let us "so much the more" enter into our chambers and shut the door, and pray to our Father Who seeth in secret, and we shall soon see the blessing coming openly upon the missionaries, missions, rulers, and peoples of Egypt and Ethiopia. May we be strengthened with might by His Spirit in the inner man for this "work" of believing prayer!

Brethren, the time is short!

The Lord has promised to heal Egypt (Is. xix. 22.); but for this He will be enquired of by His believing people.

Within the past few weeks this work of "healing" has been commenced before the eyes of the whole world by the overthrow of the Khalifa and his legions of oppressors, and thus the Central Soudan and Upper Egypt, for more than 2,000 miles down the course of the Nile from the shores of the Mediterranean, have been opened to the Gospel as never before in the history of that ancient land.

The flag of a Christian nation now floats over that vast region. HOW LONG SHALL IT BE ERE THE BANNER OF THE CROSS WAVE WITH EVERY BREEZE OVER THAT ONCE DESOLATE LAND?

CHAPTER II.

"The Labourers."

PRESENT GOSPEL EFFORTS IN EGYPT.

These who "*have borne the burden and the heat of the day.*"—MATT. xx. 12.

"*The harvest truly is plenteous, but* THE LABOURERS *are few; pray ye therefore the Lord of the harvest, that He will send forth labourers into His harvest.*"—MATT. ix. 37, 38.

"A little Sanctuary" art Thou to me,
  O Jesus, best Beloved! I live with Thee,
  My heart has found its everlasting home,
  Its sure abiding place where'er I roam.

"A little Sanctuary" art Thou to me!
  Amongst the heathen, where I dwell with Thee;
  Beneath Thy shadow, folded 'neath Thy wing,
  In deep content my song of praise I sing.

"A little Sanctuary" wert Thou to me
  *When home was left behind, and tremblingly
  I launched upon the deep*, it was to feel
  The pressure of Thine arms around me steal.

"A little Sanctuary" wert Thou indeed,
  *When in a distant land the precious seed
  Was sown in tears.* Ah, then, how more than sweet
  That "secret place," that refuge at Thy feet!

"A little Sanctuary" art Thou to me!
  All joyfully I pitch my tent with Thee,

Or ready still to journey at Thy Word—
"In Thee" I "live and move," most blesséd Lord.

"A little Sanctuary" art Thou to me!
I always am "at home" on land or sea;
Alone, yet never lonely now, I prove
The "Hundredfold," Lord Jesus, in Thy love!

"A little Sanctuary" art Thou to me;
Thus may I evermore "dwell deep" in Thee,
And daily praise for blessed foretaste given
(In doing of Thy will) of "Days of Heaven."

THE work of **The American United Presbyterian Mission** is "as a light that shineth in a dark place." Long before the British occupation, when the people still groaned under their oppressive burdens, these heroic American friends were seeking to spread the knowledge of Christ. Many of them have been faithful unto death, and have worked on through the heat and through cholera, and through danger and persecution, and we thank and praise God for their labours.

They began work in Egypt in 1854, and have gone stedfastly on for forty-four years. At first a station in Cairo, then three years later in Alexandria. In 1865, at Asioot, a large town on the Nile, which was destined to become a most important centre in Upper Egypt. In 1866, in the Faiyum, situated in the Western Desert, away from the Nile, but of very ancient fertility, owing to the water being brought by a canal from the river through the hills and forming Lake Moeris.

And so the work went on step by step through many important towns and villages, until at the present time they have 197 mission stations throughout the country. In only a few of these are there white missionaries, the greater part of them are carried on by native helpers.

The staff of the American Mission at present consists of about 50 missionaries, including wives; and of these about two-thirds have mastered the Arabic language sufficiently to speak to the people. It is a hard tongue, and some of those who have been in the country longest still continue to learn.

The native Egyptians among whom mission work is carried on are, for the most part, either Moslems or Copts. The proportion of the former to the latter is about ten to one. The local government is Mohammedan. The customs and habits of the people are Mohammedan. Even the so-called Christians and Jews have, to a large extent, adopted the sociology of the Moslems. Friday is the weekly day of rest, and Moslem holidays are those kept by the Government. The treatment of women in the home is practically the same with the Copt and the Moslem. The opinion that they are naturally inferior to the men, and were created for the men's pleasure, ease, or profit is almost universal. Ignorance of the way of salvation is nearly the same among Copts, who have not been subject to Protestant influences, as among the Moslems. The former know Christ as the son of Mary; but of salvation by the grace of God through belief in a crucified Saviour, of regeneration by the Holy Spirit, of Christian life in Christ, and the indissoluble connection between true faith and a pure life of obedience, they seem as ignorant as the followers of Mohammed. Bearing the name of Christians, and being the lineal descendants of the primitive Church of Christ in Egypt, the Copts are specially dear to the hearts of all true Christians. They have a zeal, but it is not according to knowledge. They are seeking for righteousness by fasting, by repeating psalms, by keeping feasts, by building churches, but they do not seek it where it is to be found. They, like the Mohammedans, are sinners needing a Saviour. The missionary work is to tell them of Him who is the propitiation for the sins of the whole world—Mohammedan, corrupt Christian, heathen—and has issued to the Church the great commission—"Go ye into all the world and preach the Gospel to every creature."

Very early in the history of the American Mission they saw the necessity of training natives to be workers for Christ in this land. To secure this end there must be, first, primary schools, where, from the earliest years, the principles and practices of our holy religion would be taught, and where habits and customs so numerous and so utterly inconsistent with the Christianity of God's Word would be rooted up. Then the higher schools, where the elements of the sciences would be learned, seemed also necessary in order to meet the questions continually arising from contact with residents and travellers from the West. Then, too, the theological school for the special training of those young men, who, after passing through the primary schools and academy, were moved to consecrate their lives to the service of Christ and the salvation of sinners. The primary schools, numbering now over 150, with an attendance of about 8,000 pupils, have only a nominal connection with the Mission, and are, for the most part parochial schools in connection with the congregations, or under the supervision of intelligent natives, and mostly at the expense of the natives themselves. The others are the higher schools, including the college at Asyut, in which the main object is the superior training of workers for the evangelization of Egypt. Many are trained who seek employment in Government and in the various branches of business; but without these training institutions, they could not have the workers whom they so much need. But the great reason for encouraging education and employing this method of carrying out in spirit the great commission, is to secure thereby, trained, intelligent, and pious workers.

Perhaps more than any other mission in the East, the American United Presbyterian Mission have used the distribution of books as a means of reaching the people with the Gospel. The whole of the Nile Valley, from Alexandria up to the first cataract, is now divided among nearly thirty colporteurs, who are constantly plying their vocation, carrying along every street, and into every village and town, copies of the Scriptures in the language of the people, and many other books such as "The Pilgrim's Progress," Baxter's "Call to the Unconverted," "The Work of the Spirit," "The Only Way," and controversial books on "Mohammedanism, and Romanism, and Copticism," etc. Bible-women have visited the women, and colporteurs have carried the Bible into the villages until now there is such a network of agencies in connection with this blessed Mission spreading throughout the country that surely, though quietly, the Gospel is finding its way.

Their chief efforts have been directed to the Copts, and it is

EGYPTIAN DONKEY BOYS, WITH MOHAMMEDAN SAYING HIS PRAYERS.

they who form the little churches and fill the schools, about four-fifths of the children being Coptic and Jewish, the remaining one-fifth are Moslems. But it has been felt that until the Mohammedan population could see real Christian lives, lived by those who were called Christians, that words were of little use.

Many look forward to the day—may it be very near! when Copts, filled with the Spirit of God, shall bear witness of the Lord Jesus in life and in word to their Moslem neighbours.

We earnestly ask all who read these pages to join us in praying for a special outpouring of the Holy Ghost on all the Copts in Egypt. There are some most blessed souls among them; and as they have for more than twelve hundred years suffered from their Moslem rulers and persecutors, and have still held on to their faith in Jesus, the Son of God, it would be glorious to see them once more a living Church, and a channel and instrument of blessing to their Mohammedan neighbours.

God bless the American Mission!

Although their adherents have been chiefly Copts, they have never ceased to try to win the Mohammedans, and during the forty-four years of labour they have had about sixty converts from Mohammed to Christ, sixty whom they have known, but the number of unknown ones whose names are written in heaven is doubtless far larger. They have been told sometimes of the death of a relation, and have heard the hint dropped that it was because he was suspected of becoming a Christian. They have seen the work of grace beginning in the hearts of the children, and then they have lost sight of them. "We are sure God answers prayer." For the last three or four years all the missionaries have agreed together to pray for the Moslems of Egypt at 9 o'clock every night, and we believe the time is near when a flood-tide of blessing will come, and all through the land confession will be made of faith in the Lord Jesus Christ.

* * *

The other missions at work in Egypt are still comparatively in their early days, except **The Scotch Mission**, which has had a most prosperous school in Alexandria for the last forty years. It belongs to the Established Church of Scotland, and is so well known and highly regarded that a large number of the European inhabitants of Alexandria have themselves been educated there, and now send their children to the schools. Out of the fees of the higher schools they are able to carry on a poor school for Moslem children who do not pay anything. We do thank God for these schools.

✷ ✷ ✷

The Church Missionary Society is at work in Cairo, where they have had a station for the last ten years. They have good schools for both boys and girls, and a Medical Mission and hospital at Old Cairo. The staff consists of twenty-one missionaries, including wives and those on furlough, and we trust that this number will soon be largely increased. The Mission has been anxious not to overlap the work of the American Mission, and therefore looks forward to planting new stations in the new provinces up the Nile that are now coming under the Egyptian flag. For all these we are responsible, and may God raise up and lead forth from Great Britain and Ireland men and women who will give their lives to win the long-oppressed peoples of Dongola, Berber, and Khartoum!

The following notes, culled from the reports of C.M.S. Missionaries in Egypt, are full of interest, and give a vivid picture of the joys and triumphs, as well as the difficulties and discouragements of the work :—

" Before I begin to tell you of what I have been doing during the eight months I have been out here I should like to *say how much we need more workers.* There are many houses which my Bible-women and I could visit much more frequently if only we had time, and there are whole districts where occasional visits have been paid which are simply waiting for ladies to come and work in them.

" I want a school for the poor Fellahin children very badly. There are so many bright-faced girls, too dirty and ragged and poor to come to school with our better class children, who could easily be gathered in and taught to know the story of the Saviour Who loves them, *but no one comes out to care for them.*

"Our work with the older women is slow, because they cannot see for themselves whether 'those things are so,' and they forget much of what we tell them between one visit and the next. *This is a time of special opportunity for English Christians in Egypt, is it not? And if we do not take advantage of it, shall we not before long—at least in the 'day of the Lord'— have to be sorry for it?*

GAMES OUTSIDE CAFÉ.

"The Sunday Services and week-day meetings are better attended than ever, and a good number of Moslems come to both. One young man, the son of a Bey, a brother is specially interested in. He says he is sure the young man is a believer, but his father is so afraid of his son becoming a Christian that he keeps him almost a prisoner in the house, and even holds him by the hand when he is out walking or driving. He used to come to the meetings, but lately his father has prevented him from doing so. He, however, still reads the Bible, which he keeps in a secret place so that it may not be taken from him. May God enable him one day to confess Christ openly! This is no easy matter here in Egypt in the midst of Moslem relations and friends. One young student at the Al Azhar University I know of, who would fain confess Christ, but, he asks, *will the English Government guarantee his life if he does?*

"In one house we found all the women sitting on the ground together, watching a little boy who lay dying. The poor mother sat apart from the rest, rocking herself backwards and forwards in her grief. It was a great joy to find they would listen as we told them of the resurrection and the life of the Lord Jesus. Several of these same women used to refuse to hear anything of the Gospel, saying to the Bible-woman, 'You are a Nazarene; it is wickedness for us to listen to you.'

"We have a class for the ragged girls on Sunday afternoons. From twelve to eighteen of them attend pretty regularly, and I could easily get more if I had room for them. At first they could only be got to come by giving them sweets, and rags to make dolls of, but now most of them seem to like to learn, and they behave wonderfully well, as a rule, considering that they know nothing of day-school manners.

"In spite of all drawbacks some of the women are learning to listen eagerly to the story of the Saviour's love. I have a room now in the back street in which my Bible-woman is living, and we are getting some of them to come and sit with us on Friday afternoons. It can hardly be called a 'meeting' yet, but at least we give an opportunity of hearing more to any who really want to learn.

"One poor woman told us sorrowfully the other day that these things were hard to her, and that our words went in at one side of her head and out at the other. If they could only be learning day by day instead of just now and then!

"Cholera broke out in Old Cairo, and what we feared came upon us. Alexandria had already suffered some time. Cholera, having once begun, soon made rapid progress, and each day we kept hearing of more and more deaths, till at last one day there were fifty cholera cases here, a great many for a comparatively small place. The Government carts bearing the sick, were constantly passing our house on the way to the cholera hospital, which had been hastily erected close to our new C.M.S. buildings; funerals were always going past, too, with their mourners, and one seemed to hear nothing but wailing and shrieking for the dead. When we were ordered to close the school I was free for visiting, and spent most of my time going round to the children's homes, preaching sanitation as well as the Gospel; insisting, as far as I could, on cleanliness and the use of disinfectants. It was quite encouraging when two or three actually did what you begged of them. One great difficulty was to persuade them to boil the water; it was as God gave it to them, and they were sure the doctors put poison into the water that was specially pumped from the river. Others were sure that if they drank the water they would get the cholera, not prevent it, for the doctors were going about trying to increase the cholera. Many foolish stories were going about, all of them against the doctors, who were almost working night and day to prevent the poor ignorant people from destroying themselves by their carelessness. One day I was visiting the home of a former school-girl, and there I found her married sister very ill with cholera, and all the family determined not to have a doctor. What was I to do? I had medicine in my pocket, but was rather afraid if the woman took it and died, which she was very likely to do, I might be blamed. After prayer, I offered it to her, and to my surprise she at once drank some, and I left the bottle with them. To my great joy and thankfulness she made a rapid recovery. The cholera time was a great opportunity of getting to know some of the people more intimately than before, and some were so grateful for visits when, as they said, their Mohammedan friends would not come near them, that they gladly listened to our Gospel message. Indeed, you felt it was a very solemn fact that some you were speaking to might never hear such words again.

"Since our return, in August, I have been ill twice, through trying to do more than I have strength for. But what is to be done when we are so short-handed? HOW CAN OUR BRETHREN IN ENGLAND GO ON PRAYING FOR MISSIONS TO MOSLEMS, AND YET DO SO VERY LITTLE TOWARDS THEIR CONVERSION?

THEY CERTAINLY CAN EXPECT LITTLE ANSWER TO THEIR PRAYERS. MAY THE LORD GIVE THE CHURCH AT HOME, NOT MERELY A MISSIONARY ENTHUSIASM, BUT A MISSIONARY SPIRIT, FOR WHERE THE SPIRIT LEADS THE BODY MUST GO."

* * *

The **North Africa Mission** have a station in Alexandria and also in Rosetta. Their staff consists of ten workers and some native assistants. They have a school in one of the native quarters of the town, and lately, during nine months, a number of intelligent Moslems have been coming night after night to the Mission Hall to listen to the Gospel. There is much need for workers among the villages of the Delta, and we trust this Mission may be able to plant many little stations in them. Two ladies live about a mile from Rosetta, the only Protestant missionaries in that part, and the people of the little town are gradually losing their prejudices and bringing their children to be taught. There are continual opportunities of talking to them alone or in little groups. It is an unnoticed work carried on by these two sisters alone, but we are sure it might be multiplied indefinitely among all these small towns and villages. It is easy for two ladies to live together, and work among the people round them.

The following extracts are taken from an account of an itinerating journey by two of the North Africa Missionaries, made in the villages and towns of the Delta :—

"We visited the surrounding villages. In the first, while speaking of the power and grace of the Lord Jesus to some men at their work, the women near by became fanatical, thinking, we suppose, we should bring some unknown evil to them and their families, and after we had left caused one of the men who had received a Gospel leaflet to run after us and return it. When he came to us he was full of excitement, and begged us not to be angry, and kissed us several times.

"After a long walk, under brilliant sunshine, we arrived at another village. Here we first conversed with a group of old men, one of whom was busily making string by a very simple process from the raw cotton; then made our way to another group, among whom we sold a complete copy of the Scriptures and the Psalms of David. In the absence of the Omda we were welcomed by his substitute, who ordered his servant, clad in an old sack with holes for his neck and arms, to set before us coffee, bread, and cream, which were very refreshing after our long walk. On our return we met a typical fellah or herdsman in charge of some young bulls. We sat down by his side in the fields, and began to speak with him, and soon others came near. An Arab girl brought us a loaf of native bread and plucked some green leaves such as the fellah eats. We ate with them, which gave great pleasure, so much so that they wanted us to go with them to their village, but the day was far spent, so we hastened back to our bachelor quarters. Very few of the Fellahin can read, or even understand the language of the books. But they are learning the meaning of English freedom and are willing to be taught.

"On the Tuesday following we found ourselves in the Moslem village of Saft, lying north-west from Ziftch, having a population of 6,000, no railway station, no telegraph or post office, or other sign of modern civilization. Our meals had to be eaten in the open shop of the Greek provision dealer, exposed to the gaze of the natives, to whom we seemed to be curios, and his loft above the shop became our bed-room, which he kindly allowed us to share with him. There is no school here but a large number of open-faced boys about ten years of age. We went about the village with our books. A Sheikh who was also a shopkeeper purchased several copies. A brother Sheikh passing was asked his opinion, and when he had intimated that such books were not for such as he the books were left in our hands. However, he re-purchased the books afterwards by means of his boy, who visited us at our resting place. We also conversed with a group of men, among whom was another Sheikh, but less bigoted. He read in a loud clear voice the 6th, 7th, and 8th chapters of St. Matthew's Gospel to about twenty men, and commended the truths. Afterwards he brought the Omda and leading men of the village to our lodging to visit us, and we were invited to return the visit.

"The next morning after breakfast we visited the Omda again, who accepted a complete copy of the Scriptures."

* * *

There are two or three other quiet efforts for good going on in Egypt that are little known. The Dutch have a small mission at Kalioob, where they have worked on patiently for many years. Mr. Peter Rudolph, a Jewish Missionary, has worked in Alexandria among the Jews and for the poor of the city. He has been so much respected that the merchants and others have built a house called the "Asile Rudolph," where he lives and cares for the poor and suffering.

Mr. Locke, at Port Said, has a Home for Merchant Seamen, a most needed refuge in a very needy spot, and there is also a Home in Alexandria. There are Soldiers' Homes in both Alexandria and Cairo, the last-mentioned only lately started, and already it promises by God's good hand upon it to grow into a large and valuable institution. It may be interesting to relate how this is being brought about.

Mrs. Todd Osborne opened a small Soldiers' Home in Cairo last April, the need being a very real one. The premises were too small, and she had been searching for something more spacious and suitable. The Alhambra Music Hall, within a few minutes' walk of Shepheard's Hotel, the centre of the city, was offered for sale at the price of £3,000. Land is very difficult to buy in Cairo, being so valuable, and Mrs. Todd Osborne felt that this building was large enough to be available both for a Soldiers' Home and a Hall for Meetings. After much prayer that God would send the money, and that it might be given from Himself in answer to prayer, the matter was mentioned at a meeting held for Egypt after the close of the Keswick Convention.

Such real sympathy was felt, and God so stirred some hearts present, that one friend gave £1,000 towards it the same night. The next day another friend promised £1,000, and a month later a third sent the remaining £1,000 needed. Truly all who know Cairo will rejoice and thank God, feeling that He has some most special favour towards the undertaking, and has great blessings in store for it. If He gives the further means necessary, Mrs. Todd Osborne will add a Workers' Home to the rest of the buildings, making a much needed headquarters of Christian work in the midst of this great city. May God raise up a standard for Himself in Cairo!

There are some dear people who have long and faithfully served God and their fellows both in Cairo and Alexandria. These are the **German Deaconesses**, who have large and most valued Hospitals in both cities.

One far-reaching work, **The British and Foreign Bible Society**, has been going on for many years in Egypt, and though we speak of it last it would perhaps be first in God's sight and in His working.

This Society, and now **The American Bible Society**, are sowing Egypt with the Word of God. All up the Nile Valley we may find the Bible in Arabic. Portions of the Scriptures and Gospel tracts and papers in the language of the people are carried everywhere.

Still few comparatively can read, and the words need the living voice to follow them and to speak of them. It was through intensely realising this need, the need of simple and direct Gospel teaching and preaching among the Moslems of Egypt, that some who cared for the land and its people specially gave themselves to pray for it. That God would send forth men with that sole object in view, not to give themselves to medical work, although so useful in removing prejudice; not to give themselves to school work, although that is urgently required, but to devote their whole life and energies to carry the Gospel Message through the country.

We believe that it was in answer to this prayer, and because the prayer itself was God's own desire and prompting, that He has called out and separated and taken the little group of young men from Belfast to Egypt.

"Set Apart."

"Know that the Lord hath set apart him that is godly for Himself."—PSALM iv. 3.

    Set apart for Jesus!
    Is not this enough,
    Though the desert prospect
    Open wild and rough?
Set apart for His delight,
    Chosen for His holy pleasure,
    Sealed to be His holy treasure!
Could we choose a nobler joy?—and would we if we might?

    Set apart to serve Him,
    Ministers of light,
    Standing in His presence,
    Ready day or night!
Chosen for His service blest,
    He would have us always willing
    Like the angel hosts, fulfilling
Swiftly and rejoicingly, each recognised behest.

    Set apart to praise Him,
    Set apart for this!
    Have the blessèd angels
    Any truer bliss?
Soft the prelude, though so clear;
    Isolated tones are trembling;
    But the chosen choir, assembling,
Soon shall sing together, while the universe shall hear.

    Set apart to love Him,
    And His love to know!
    Not to waste affection
    On a passing show.
Called to give Him life and heart,
    Called to pour the hidden treasure,
    That none other claims to measure,
Into His belovèd hand! thrice-blessèd "set apart!"

    Set apart for ever
    For Himself alone!
    Now we see our calling
    Gloriously shown!
Owning, with no secret dread,
    This our holy separation,
    Now the crown of consecration
Of the Lord our God shall rest upon our willing head!

CHAPTER III.

The Ordination of the "Pierced Hands."

"*As they ministered to the Lord, and fasted, the Holy Ghost said, Separate me Barnabas and Saul for the work whereunto I have called them. So they, being sent forth by the Holy Ghost, departed. . . .*"—ACTS xiii. 2, 4.

From the glory and the gladness,
  From His secret place;
From the rapture of His presence
  From His radiant face
Christ, the Son of God, hath sent me
  Through the midnight lands;
MINE THE MIGHTY ORDINATION
  OF THE PIERCED HANDS.

But I tell you I have seen Him,
  God's belovèd Son;
From His lips have learnt the mystery
  He and His are one.
There, as knit into the body
  Every joint and limb,
We, His ransomed, His belovèd,
  We are one with Him.

Mine the message grand and glorious,
  Strange unsealed surprise—
That the goal is God's Belovèd,
  Christ in Paradise.
    Glory to His Name!
    Glory to His Name!
Yes, the goal is God's Belovèd,
    Glory to His Name!

THE object of this Missionary Story is to shew forth the glory of the Lord, in calling out and sending forth a band of His servants from Belfast and Glasgow to the land

THE ORDINATION OF THE "PIERCED HANDS." 31

of Egypt. The following is a brief account of the two lines of leading, quite distinct and unknown to each other in their origin, but which were destined, in His providence, to be united as a distinct answer to prayer, into one stream of blessing.

We first give the story of one whose interest in Egypt for many years past led her to pray that "the Lord would send forth labourers into the harvest"; and then the brief statement issued by the members of the band to their friends, on the eve of their sailing for their future sphere of labour for the Master.

* * *

"When He saw the multitudes, He was moved with compassion for them, because they were distressed and scattered as sheep not having a shepherd. Then saith He unto His disciples, The harvest truly is plenteous, but the labourers are few. Pray ye therefore the Lord of the harvest, that He send forth labourers into His harvest" (Matt. ix. 36—38, R.V.).

Was it even so again in Egypt? Was it that the Lord had compassion on the scattered and straying multitudes, and that He bid His disciples pray?

About two years and a half ago, the intensity of the need and the scanty supply of labourers, and still more, the hardness and unyieldingness of the soil on which the seed was sown, led a few of God's children to form a Prayer Union especially for Egypt. They prayed for the land and its people; for the Jews, Moslems, and Copts; for the missionaries and mission schools; for the Word of God carried throughout the country; and for the British soldiers stationed there.

They took for their text, "Continuing daily with one accord in prayer" for Egypt; and truly they can look up with thankfulness and say, "We have proved God answers prayer." Each Mission can tell of encouragement. There is no feeling of hopelessness with regard to the conversion of the Moslems. The American Missionaries can tell remarkable instances of the work of the Spirit of God in their schools. The North Africa Missionaries can tell of wonderful readiness to hear the

Word, and of open doors, where a few years ago there was hostility. The increase of education is bringing large numbers of the people into the possibility of reading for themselves, and on all sides there is hope and faith and expectation.

It seemed to some of us who shared the work in deep heart-sympathy that there were two things to pray for unceasingly, until the answer came :—THAT GOD WOULD OPEN THE WINDOWS OF HEAVEN AND POUR OUT HIS SPIRIT ON ALL HIS OWN PEOPLE IN EGYPT, AND THAT HE WOULD THRUST FORTH MORE LABOURERS INTO HIS VINEYARD.

The cry of those belonging to the Church Missionary Society was, "Send us men!" The work was growing, and there were open doors but no one to go. Instead of increasing, their numbers could hardly be sustained. The great and urgent need, which pressed on many hearts, was that of men to give themselves wholly to Evangelistic work. At every station the school work was going on. In two or three centres Medical Missions were prospering, and the work amongst the women in the large towns was cared for ; but so few, so very few men who knew Arabic could give themselves up to preach Christ to the Moslems. And yet they could be reached. They were perfectly willing to listen, but there was hardly anyone to go amongst them and devote their lives to this purpose. It was through knowing this, and through the sight of the multitudes sitting in darkness and in the shadow of death, that a friend of the Missionaries, Miss Annie Van Sommer, took the matter specially to God in prayer. She prayed for men to come forward for this one work—To take the Gospel to the Moslems.

After waiting for some time on God about it, the opportunity came for her to attend the Students' Summer Conference, held that year at Curbar. She was allowed a quarter of an hour to tell the Students of the needs of Egypt. For three weeks preceding the Conference one prayer was in her heart and on her lips, night and day—that God would send out seven men from that Students' gathering to Egypt.

When the time came, before one word had been said about it, God brought her into contact with a little group of young men who had come from Belfast. She was told they had all

THE ORDINATION OF THE "PIERCED HANDS." 33

heard the Lord's call to the Foreign Mission field; that they were prepared to leave all and follow Jesus; and that four out of a little group of six had come to Curbar, asking God to shew them there, where they were to go.

When first she was told this story, after just coming into contact with the little group, Miss Van Sommer took it earnestly to the Lord in prayer, asking Him to shew her if these were the men for whom she had been praying. Her only thought had been to reinforce the Missions out there, but this little band of young men felt they were to go depending on the Lord alone for support, and looking to Him direct as their Head and Leader.

This seemed to open unknown and unexpected possibilities and even dangers, and Miss Van Sommer felt she dared not tell them of Egypt, unless the Lord would give her a very distinct assurance from Himself that the thing was from Him, and that it was His doing, not hers, or theirs. As she prayed on through the night, in her lodgings near Curbar, all fears were taken away. She felt it was out of her hands into His, and that it was God Himself who had prepared it all, and had His own plan that He would carry out; and that He had only brought her there to give His message to them.

In the early dawn of the following morning she looked at "Daily Light" for the day, the 31st of July, and read, "I have given Him for a witness to the people, a LEADER and COMMANDER to the people" (Is. lv. 4).

A few hours later the opportunity was given to meet the four who were at Curbar. They all sat down in a field together and spoke of Egypt. There was no wish to persuade or to accomplish a desire; the only thought in every heart was, "Is this the Lord's call to the little band from Belfast? Does He want them in Egypt?"

It was put unitedly into His hands, and they all agreed to separate and wait upon God about it, until His will was clear to them. The difficulties of the situation were faced. There was no certain prospect of support from any quarter. Most of them were in business, and were prepared to part with it, and use in common whatever they possessed. They belonged to different denominations, but were so much one in spirit this was no barrier.

For the next two or three days much time was spent apart in prayer, seeking clear guidance for the future, and before the whole party broke up and separated the conviction was deepened in the mind of each one that Egypt was the "vineyard" to which God was saying to him, "Son, go work to-day," and each had gladly responded, "I go."

The words which had been used as a bond that drew them all together were—"These are they which follow the Lamb whithersoever He goeth" (Rev. xiv. 4).

In the testimonies which were given at their farewell meetings, it will be seen that this was a personal, individual call to each one separately, so clear and strong that more than one felt that if none of the others went he was himself to go to Egypt; and, as they all saw this in each other, they felt it was no impulse or imagination, but a real purpose for life which had come from heaven.

At the time, the first thing to be done was to go back to Belfast and tell the other brethren, and then the harder task of telling home friends, and the beginning of the severance of home ties. All went quietly forward. No word was said about money, but every need was supplied. One great friend of the little band, who afterwards accompanied them on the voyage, had also at a distance been praying alone that their way might be made clear to them at Curbar, and as he prayed the words came with startling emphasis to his mind, "Out of Egypt have I called my Son." A little later, when he met some of the party, and they told him they knew where they were to go, he said, "Tell me first, is it Egypt?"

The seventh member of the party joined them before the time came to go forward, and then as each step to be taken confronted them it was found that difficulties disappeared, and there was light on the way. One of the number went first, four followed shortly afterwards, and at the present time the remaining two are about to join the other five, thus making complete the party of seven. Whether others are ever to join them or not they do not know, but they are sure that the same

Lord who has gone before them, and who performeth all things for them, will make His will clear in times to come as He has done in the past.

When the little band landed in Alexandria, He guided them to a house, which is for the present their home. He supplied them with Arabic teachers, and helped them through the first days of the difficult language. He gave them the loving friendship of missionaries on every side, and He has given them the joy of being His messengers to needy souls around them.

We would "show forth Thy lovingkindness in the morning, and Thy faithfulness every night. For Thou, Lord, hast made me glad through Thy work: I will triumph in the works of Thy hands" (Ps. xcii. 2, 4).

And thus while the Holy Spirit was laying the burden of Egypt on the heart of our sister in England, He was preparing the men in Ireland for the fulfilment of that prayer, as indicated in the following statement and the "Life Stories" given in succeeding chapter.

EGYPT MISSION BAND.

BELFAST,
December, 1897.

BELOVED IN THE LORD JESUS CHRIST,

You may have heard that we propose (D.V.) to sail for Egypt in the coming year, for the purpose of undertaking mission work in that country as the Lord may guide us. Feeling, however, the great need of earnest believing prayer on our behalf, and with a view to obtaining your co-operation in this way, we desire to tell you shortly how we come to be going out and what we hope to do if God will.

In the early spring of 1896, the Lord began to draw together a band of young men in Belfast for prayer and work, chiefly in the open air. Most of us had received very definite blessing either directly or indirectly through the Keswick Convention.

GENERAL VIEW OF KESWICK.

The little band, which was entirely interdenominational in its character, grew until it numbered thirteen, and in February last at one of our weekly half-nights of prayer, those of us who were present were constrained by the Spirit of God in humble dependence on Him to sign our names to the following pledge :—

"LORD, I AM AT THY DISPOSAL FOR FOREIGN MISSIONARY WORK AS SOON AND WHEREVER THOU CALLEST ME."

The Lord had been dealing with some of us for some time previously, as to the needs of the heathen world, but this seemed to add definiteness to what had hitherto been but vague. We felt we were given away to God for this particular work in a manner we had not been before. He took us at our word on that 16th February and began to slowly unfold His plan, but it was not until the month of April that He revealed His purpose of sending out a band of seven to work together. One after another the Holy Spirit separated six of us, dealing with each one individually, and without collusion on our part, bringing our hearts into line with His will and with one another. Those whom He "separated" joined together in prayer for the others that were still required to complete the band, and that He might make known to us the sphere in which we were to labour. After two months of constant prayer and waiting on God for guidance, He led four of us to the Students' Conference at Curbar. Here the needs of Egypt were laid before us by Miss Van Sommer, who had lately returned from there, and who had come to the Conference as she herself said, after weeks of earnest prayer that God would send forth seven men to work in that country. We had much prayer about the matter unitedly and alone, and it was made quite clear to all individually that the call was from the Lord and ought to be obeyed. We have since received abundant confirmation of the leading, and now the band of seven, as indicated by the Lord in April last, is complete.

The sphere of our work will be Egypt, our desire being to strengthen the hands of those already working there, some of whom have sent us a warm welcome. In the first instance, it is our thought to settle down in Alexandria, where we shall have (D.V.) a small headquarters station. Some of us may find open doors for work among the Jews, Maltese, Greeks, and others, while those of us, who believe we are to go to the Moslems, will press on into the interior as soon as the way is made plain. The population of Egypt is about 9,000,000, mostly Mohammedans, scattered over a strip of country on either bank of the Nile, extending for a distance of about 1,200 miles, all open for work, but only occupied by Mission Stations for about half this distance. The new railway which is being pushed on towards Khartoum, will afford such facilities for preaching the Gospel, as constitutes in itself a trumpet call to the Church of God to go in and possess the land for Jesus. In Egypt alone, there is a population of fully 120,000 to each Protestant Missionary, so that there is ample scope for us in helping the workers who are labouring in the field, and in breaking up new ground.

In addition to what we have just mentioned, there is a special need why this enterprise should be encircled with mighty prevailing prayer. We are going into the very citadel of Mohammedanism, upon which nothing but the mighty power of the Holy Spirit will avail to make any impression. In the University of Al Azhar, Cairo, there are from five to ten thousand students preparing for the propagation of the religion of Islam throughout the world.

Such, roughly, is the need. We believe that "with God all things are possible," and that the Gospel is still "the power of God unto salvation to everyone that believeth," whether Moslem or heathen. We have the Lord's own promise waiting to be pleaded—"The Lord shall be known to Egypt, and the Egyptians shall know the Lord in that day, . . ." (Is. xix. 21). Will you join us, "helping together by prayer," to hasten "that day?" "All things whatsoever ye shall ask in prayer, believing ye shall receive." We want definite, believing, continual intercession.

We are going forth in absolute dependence on the Holy Spirit of God, conscious of our own utter nothingness, but also of His mighty power, being confident of this one thing that He who has led us thus far will perfect that which concerneth us and will preserve us unto His Heavenly Kingdom.

Beloved, "continue steadfastly in prayer, watching therein

with thanksgiving; withal praying for us also, that God may open unto us a door for the Word, to speak the mystery of Christ," and that we "may be blameless and harmless, the sons of God without rebuke."

Yours in Christ Jesus,

WM. BRADLEY,
J. MARTIN CLEAVER,
FREDK. G. COONEY,
JOHN GORDON LOGAN,
GEORGE SWAN,
T. EDWARD SWAN,
ELIAS H. THOMPSON.

"*Brethren, pray for us.*"—1.THESS. v. 25.

THE SOVEREIGNTY OF GOD.

"*Be still, and know that I am God : I will be exalted among the heathen, I will be exalted in the earth.*"—PSALM xlvi. 10.

God Almighty! King of nations! earth Thy footstool, heaven Thy throne!
Thine the greatness, power, and glory; Thine the kingdom, Lord, alone;
Life and death are in Thy keeping, and Thy will ordaineth all,
From the armies of Thy heavens to an unseen insect's fall.

Reigning, guiding, all-commanding, ruling myriad worlds of light;
Now exalting, now abasing, none can stay Thy hand of might,
Working all things by Thy power, by the counsel of Thy will;
Thou art God! enough to know it, and to hear Thy word—" be still."

In Thy sovereignty rejoicing, we Thy children bow and praise,
For we know that kind and loving, just and true are all Thy ways,
While Thy heart of sovereign mercy and Thine arm of sovereign might,
For our great and strong salvation, in Thy sovereign grace unite.

CHAPTER IV.

Deliverance and Translation.

LIFE STORIES.

"*Giving thanks unto the Father, which hath made us meet to be partakers of the inheritance of the saints in light:*

"*Who hath delivered us from the power of darkness, and hath translated us into the kingdom of His dear Son.*"—COL. i. 12, 13.

"GO YE FORTH."

From the brightness of the glory,
 "Go ye forth," He said;
 "Heal the sick, and cleanse the lepers,
 Raise the dead.

"Freely give I thee the treasure,
 Freely give the same;
 Take no store of gold or silver—
 Take My Name.

"Thou art fitted for the journey,
 How so long it be;
 Thou shalt come, unworn, unwearied,
 Back to Me.

"Thou shalt tell Me in the glory
 All that thou hast done,
 Setting forth alone; returning
 Not alone.

"Thou shalt bring the ransomed with thee,
 They with songs shall come
 As the golden sheaves of harvest,
 Gathered home."

"*But ye shall receive power, after that the Holy Ghost is come upon you: and ye shall be witnesses unto Me both in Jerusalem, and in all Judæa, and in Samaria, and unto the uttermost part of the earth.*"—ACTS i. 8.

"*As Thou hast sent Me into the world, even so have I also sent them into the world.*"—JOHN xvii. 18.

WILLIAM BRADLEY.

"*And they overcame him by the blood of the Lamb, and by the word of their testimony; and they loved not their lives unto the death.*"—REV. xii. 11.

"The dying thief rejoiced to see
That fountain in his day;
And there may I, though vile as he,
Wash all my sins away."

WILLIAM BRADLEY.

BORN of Christian parents, I was brought up in the fear of the Lord, and sent regularly to the Sabbath school and to church. As a Presbyterian I had to learn the Shorter Catechism and texts of Scripture; this duty I always hated, and shall never forget receiving many whippings from a godly schoolmaster because I objected to learn the 55th chapter of Isaiah. Thus beaten into me I shall always remember it. A part of the 8th chapter of Romans was learnt in the same way, and I praise God for the knowledge of these to-day. At the age of 15 I left the Sunday school to attend the City Y.M.C.A. Bible class for men, and then later went to church only once on the Sabbath day. Mixing with worldly companions, the love for sport and amusement seized me, and this, with business, made me very indifferent to the claims of God.

My godly mother was greatly attached to me; she talked and read and prayed with me. I did not like to disobey her, and but for her influence I would have given up all religious restraint.

Seven years ago the Lord called my mother home after a brief illness. I realised I had lost my very best friend, and felt broken-hearted.

A year later I started to travel in England, Ireland, and Scotland for a Belfast linen house, and did my utmost in the new surroundings to satisfy myself with worldly pleasures. Then the Lord strove with me. I had promised my mother I would give my heart to the Lord, and meet her in heaven, and then, too, her prayers had called forth the Spirit's convicting power in my heart; yet for five years I yielded to the devil, who did his utmost, by way of attractions, to allure me from God.

Three years ago I was laid on my back through a strain received in athletics. This necessitated an operation which, the doctor informed me, might prove fatal. However, I made up my mind to face it at all costs. God again pressed me about my soul, but I said—"I have lived a life contrary to God, and I will not try to sneak into heaven now." So I resolved to go into hospital, and if I died I was resigned to my eternal fate. I shall never forget the third morning after the operation; the doctor being sent for, my temperature was at 106°. It was thought inflammation had set in, and my case was hopeless. The sight I had of an undone eternity I cannot forget, but the Lord had mercy on me and spared my life, and restored me to health such as I never experienced before; this was about July, 1894. From that time forward God especially dealt with me. I got sick of company and all kinds of pleasure, and began to have my eyes opened to the hollowness of the whole thing, and in looking back saw what an awful blank my life had been.

I then began to realise in '95 that God was surrounding me, and I could not get away from the Spirit's dealings (especially when I would go to bed at night), and I knew many Christians were praying much for my conversion, which increased my anxiety. I shall never forget Sunday afternoon, the 20th of October, 1895, sitting with a number of friends in one of the leading athletic club grounds, and making an appointment to go to the theatre the next night. I went that Sunday afternoon to the Y.M.C.A. Service in the Ulster Hall Annexe, and the preacher seemed to hit straight at me. I then went home, and, kneeling down, told the Lord I was a poor, lost, hell-deserving sinner, and asked Him to forgive and receive me. The next day I went to a Christian friend, who quoted me 1st John i. 9—" If we confess our sins, He is faithful and just to forgive us our sins, and to cleanse us from *all unrighteousness.*" I shouted " Hallelujah ! "

I endeavoured to follow the Lord fully, and to confess Christ; and, praise God, I received the baptism of the Holy Spirit right at the start, and then and there told my friends I had given my heart to Jesus. The Lord then spoke definitely to me about separation from the world, and led me to make a clean cut with it, and be satisfied with the companionship of Christ only. God then revealed to me the blessed communion of prayer to such an extent that words entirely fail to express the blessing.

Six months after my conversion God put a special test on my Christian profession. I was asked to go with a band of others to start a parade from the Gas Works to Ballynafeigh on Easter Monday, 1896, and then to take part in an open-air service outside the Ulster grounds, where the annual athletic meeting was being held and most of my old sporting companions present. I shall never forget the struggle I had with the devil, and as soon as I yielded to God I received His blessed peace. How I have praised Him since, for in that fiery trial, amidst all the laughs and sneers, " His right hand sustained me." I shall never forget the supreme joy that filled my soul at the close of the day; the "obedience to His revealed will" unlocked many precious promises in God's Word—" If any man willeth to do My will, he shall know of the doctrine, whether it be of God, or whether I speak from Myself." How the Lord blessed me after this, eternity alone will reveal.

My next cross was to go to the Maze Races to give out tracts and testify for Jesus. I knew this burnt other bridges behind me, but there was no longer resistance, for God was "all in all" to my soul.

The privilege of a visit to Keswick Convention brought me into closer touch with the Lord, and there, I believe, He taught me to cease from the evil habit of judging and criticising my fellow-Christians.

The Lord was increasing a burning desire to go to the heathen and tell them of Jesus, and, as I spent nights alone with God, I saw that my way was going to be made very clear, and many were the visions I had of Jesus and His cross, and sufferings for me, and visions of heaven and hell which thrilled my soul and increased my thirst for God and perishing souls.

On February 16th, 1897, God met me in a memorable halfnight of prayer and sealed my future for the Regions Beyond. I was confident from that night that my life was to be spent amongst the heathen; I knew not what field, but I sung with all my heart, "anywhere with Jesus." In April I was in England on business, and, especially when in Manchester, I felt definitely called each night to return to my hotel after business and be silent before God from 6 p.m. to 11 p.m. I could not utter words, nor did I get any special light from God, but just knelt quietly and God did His secret work in my soul. When I returned I felt constrained to go round and see my dear brother Cleaver. He told me how the Lord had been laying it on his heart and the hearts of others, that He was going to separate and send forth a band of seven young men to preach the Gospel in the Foreign Mission field; and how that if I was to be one of the number that God would make it plain; like a flash the Lord showed me that the previous nights were for preparation of soul for the news of His glorious leading, and the whole thing was opened up to me. Then I began to lay before God certain difficulties, which He cleared up for me, so my brothers and myself started to pray quietly, not so much to know where to go as to be separated by the Holy Ghost one from another, and to be made perfectly pliable to go forward, or to stay at home, and to get all the novelty of going away taken out of us, and, in short, to be entirely abandoned to God to do His will. In July we arranged to go to Curbar. On the Saturday morning we met a lady who had been praying for seven to go to Egypt. We spent that day in prayer, and then at night came the call from God to go each one alone on the mountain and deal with Him individually about the matter. I have great reason never to forget that night, as being a time when I received one of the most subtle attacks from the devil; for nearly two hours he tried to put me asleep. I held on to God till my strength was almost gone, and I was done out, then God quickened my body with new life, and put the devil to flight. He then dealt with me—"Was I willing to go alone?" and, after a hard struggle, I said, "Yes, Lord." From that till the present I have never had any doubt as to my future field of labour. It was sealed to my soul by the Holy Spirit, about 4 a.m. on Sunday morning, that it was Egypt, and all the world could not persuade me to believe otherwise. Praise God, since then the mountains have been removed, and now the way is all clear. All glory be to Jesus!

God grant that all who read this simple testimony may yield themselves entirely up to God, body, soul, and spirit, to live for the glory of Christ. Christ is all in all to my soul.

A poor sinner saved by grace.

J. MARTIN CLEAVER.

"He found him in a desert land, and in the waste howling wilderness; He led him about, He instructed him, He kept him as the apple of his eye."—DEUT. xxxii. 10.

>Jesus hath died and hath risen again,
>　　Pardon and peace to bestow ;
>Fully I trust Him ; from sin's guilty stain,
>　　Jesus saves me now.
>
>Sin's condemnation is over and gone,
>　　Jesus alone knoweth how ;
>Life and salvation my soul hath put on :
>　　Jesus saves me now.

Satan may tempt, but he never shall reign,
  That Christ will never allow;
Doubts I have buried, and this is my strain,
  " Jesus saves me now."

Resting in Jesus, abiding in Him,
  Gladly my faith can avow,—
Never again need my pathway be dim:
  Jesus saves me now.

Jesus is stronger than Satan and sin,
  Satan to Jesus must bow;
Therefore I triumph without and within:
  Jesus saves me now.

Sorrow and pain may beset me about,
  Nothing can darken my brow;
Battling in faith, I can joyfully shout:
  " Jesus saves me now."

IT is now eight years since I found the Lord Jesus Christ as my Saviour, but, sad to relate, after the first burst of zeal, the outcome of my newborn love and heartfelt gratitude to the Lord Jesus for having borne my sins in His own body on the tree, the world with its allurements crept in, and I estranged myself from my loving, tender Saviour who ceased not, however, to follow me in all my miserable wanderings from Him. Three years later found me studying in Dublin; a fellow-student,

J. MARTIN CLEAVER.

who was an out-and-out Christian, took an interest in me, and soon saw the miserable state I was in. He invited me one evening to his rooms for tea, and there pleaded with me to come back to my Saviour. He asked me if I would not allow God to give me another start? But I said, "No. I have dishonoured Him once, and do not want to do so again." Then my friend pointed out to me that it was not a question of looking into the future, but simply of trusting Jesus for the present moment. He said to me, "Don't you know that Jesus saves me *now*, and if He saves me *now*, He can save you *now*, and save you all the time." This idea of trusting Jesus for a moment at a time was a new one to me, and I answered, "I feel that I am trusting Jesus to save me *now*, to take me right back again." "Well," said he, "cannot you always keep trusting Him to save you *now*?" "Yes," I said, "I can;" and thus, very simply, the most important turning point in my life, next to my conversion, took place. God used this servant of His as an instrument whereby the joy of salvation was restored unto me. Although those three years can never be looked back upon but with regret, God overruled them to teach me the all-important lessons of the depravity of the human heart by nature, and that no good thing dwelt in me.

Returning to Belfast, after the completion of my college course, I came into contact with the work in connection with Felt Street Mission, and started to teach a Sunday school class. This work proved a great blessing to me, as I felt I learnt far more than I taught.

Up to this time my life was still more or less unsatisfactory; I longed to have deliverance from the power of sin, but sought it by effort, first by trying to put this little bit of my life right, and then that, and thus was drinking of bitter water, instead of going straight to the fountain head. So God met me again at a special mission in Felt Street. I well remember how pointed the speaker was; God seemed to have revealed to him my innermost heart, and his messages were directly for me. I used to sit close to him in the meetings, playing the organ, and he had a habit of inadvertently putting his hand almost down on my head, as he would emphasize some remark, that often went straight home to my heart, and, altogether, I felt

FELT STREET MISSION HALL, BELFAST.

DELIVERANCE AND TRANSLATION. 49

decidedly uncomfortable. Now and again he would introduce a word with regard to smoking. Up to this time I had been a smoking Christian, and this had been a cloud between my soul and God, but He gave me grace to lay aside this weight along with many others before the close of that mission, and I entered into a deeper peace, greater liberty, and a more wholehearted devotion to God. And yet I was conscious that there was still something lacking, something that, it was evident, the friend who conducted the mission had and I had not. From him I first heard of the Keswick Convention, and arranged to go there. Satan seemed to place every hindrance in my way to prevent my going, but God cleared away all obstacles, and the summer of 1895 found me there for the first time. The first day was a time of very deep heart-searching, but on the second day God met me while one of the speakers was giving a message from the words, "He healeth all thy diseases" (Psalm ciii. 3), and I there and then handed over my case absolutely into the hands of the Great Physician.

Two days later I met a brother in the Lord, whom I had occasionally met in Belfast, and was telling him what great things the Lord had done for me. He asked me—"Have you received the Holy Ghost?" I thought I had received everything I wanted, and his question was quite a surprise to me: I did want everything. So we took our Bibles, and he clearly shewed me that the gift of the Holy Ghost was the promise of the Father *for me*, and that it was a gift to be accepted in childlike faith and simplicity, in the same way as one received eternal life. We knelt down, and I prayed God to fill my soul with the Holy Ghost. The answer came immediately out of His own Word—"If ye then, being evil, know how to give good gifts unto your children, how much more shall your Heavenly Father give His Holy Spirit to them that ask Him."

After I came home the Lord began to deal with me about the Mission Field. This I believe to be the natural outcome of the filling of the Spirit, as it is written, "Ye shall receive power, after that the Holy Ghost is come upon you: and ye shall be witnesses unto Me, both in Jerusalem, and in all Judæa, and in Samaria, and unto the uttermost part of the earth." At first I put it off, but soon saw that if the peace of God in my soul was to be maintained, I must yield to Him in everything, and thus He led me on to know and follow Him more fully. The next spring God began to draw together a band of young men for work in the open air. In connection with these meetings we used to gather together for a half-night of prayer every week. These gatherings were so blessed, that soon the little band numbered about thirteen. The young men were from many different denominations, and were already engaged in active Christian work in connection with the Churches to which they belonged. During all this time I was constantly waiting upon God to know where He would have me to go. It seemed utterly impossible to me that the way would ever open, but I seemed to get it very definitely from God that I should keep myself free and wait for Him to open the door. On February 16th, 1897, at our usual half-night of prayer, God seemed to come very close and speak to our hearts. Before I went into the meeting I felt God was going to do a "separating work" that night. On comparing notes afterwards with the others, I found that most of them had had the same impression. One brother prayed that each of us might be like Gideon, and cut down our own groves, and get down low before God, that He might be free to do with us as He willed. A solemn time of heart-searching followed. It was laid on the heart of one of the members to roughly draft out on a piece of paper the following Missionary Declaration :—

"LORD, I AM AT THY DISPOSAL FOR FOREIGN MISSIONARY WORK AS SOON AND WHEREVER THOU CALLEST ME."

To this all present (thirteen in number) signed their names. From that night I felt more definitely than ever before separated unto God for Foreign Mission work.

Things went on much as usual until April, with the exception that a few days afterwards I received a call to take charge of a Mission Station in India, but had no liberty to accept it. The 25th of April is marked in my Bible as a day I shall never forget. God very definitely led me out in prayer for Foreign Missions, and gave me a wonderful

DELIVERANCE AND TRANSLATION.

assurance that He would take a Band of Seven of us out together to the Regions Beyond. God so definitely laid this on my heart, and the names of six of the seven He was going to send, that I wrote the names down in my diary with an account of how God had dealt with me. God brought the others into line with His purpose without any human intervention, and soon six of the seven were meeting as often as possible for prayer, especially praying to know the place God would have us to go, and asking that God should separate the seventh. Soon after this four of us were led to go to the Annual Conference of the "Students' Volunteer Missionary Union," at Curbar. When there we waited very definitely on God to know His purpose in sending us, and on the second day, as we were going to the meeting, we saw a friend standing on one side talking to a lady. He beckoned me to come over, and introduced me to this lady. She had prayed for years about Egypt, and had felt very definitely led of God to come to Curbar and ask for seven men for this country. We told her how God had been leading us, and that we had the assurance He was going to send seven of us out together. She then told us simply and quietly the needs of Egypt, and we left to go apart separately on to the mountain-side to spend the night alone waiting on God to know His will. Some of the others received a clear witness that this call was for them; I did not, I wanted to know very definitely whether God had been speaking, or was it my own desire. I asked God on my knees to give me a verse, and turning to open my Bible I found—"I, even I, have spoken, yea I have called him and will make his way prosperous, and I will give him to be a light to the Gentiles."

That silenced all doubt in my heart, I had God's Word for it. Thus the Lord led me and called me to follow Him to Egypt.

FRED. G. COONEY.

"He brought me up also out of an horrible pit, out of the miry clay, and set my feet upon a rock, and established my goings. And He hath put a new song in my mouth, even praise unto our God: many shall see it, and fear, and shall trust in the Lord."—PSA. xl. 2, 3.

> "Jesus, Thy blood and righteousness
> My beauty are, my glorious dress,
> 'Midst flaming worlds, in these arrayed,
> With joy shall I lift up my head."

FRED. G. COONEY.

"GIVING thanks unto the Father, Who made me meet to be a partaker of the inheritance of the saints in light; and Who delivered me out of the power of darkness, and translated me into the kingdom of the Son of His love, that I may be presented holy and without blemish and unreprovable before Him; if so be that I continue in the faith, grounded and steadfast."

Previous to my conversion, besides being under the wrath of God as a Christ-rejector, I lived solely and only for pleasure; a fast life it might well have been called, so fast that I was fully persuaded no power could pull me up.

DELIVERANCE AND TRANSLATION.

While I was in this awful condition a few of my acquaintances met together, entirely unknown to me, and pleaded with God for my conversion, and that it would occur at my sister's wedding, which was shortly to take place. A strange time, some might say, to think of such things; but God is waiting to manifest His power at all times, if He can find faithful hearts through whom to do so. I went to the wedding, and just as I was coming away—still ignorant of the fact that there were souls holding on to God for me—standing on the railway platform with my brother, who was to travel with me, I thought it would be an awful bore to have him speaking to me about my soul, but with a determination to cut him as short as possible, we took our seats in a smoking compartment alongside several loud-talking horse-dealers. Under covert of the noise my brother spoke to me of Jesus, "my Jesus," and how I had been spurning His love all my life, and as He spoke, the blessed Spirit of God bore the words home to my heart and revealed my waiting Saviour to me. While this was going on the devil was rousing himself, and then began a battle I shall never forget. I realised my position at once. Here was I, with the awful power of free-will, the loving invitation of my crucified and risen Lord pleading with that still small voice on one hand, and the devil flooding my mind with his baits and lies on the other. First he drags out his favourite, "You won't stand," then he arrays a long list of my pleasures, sinful and harmless, and winds up with "You'll have to give these up, and you can't do it"; then he passed before my mind all my worldly companions, and pictured them with a sneer on their faces, and said "You can't stand it." And many other devices he used. Through it all I saw my Saviour waiting. My will commenced to waver, and my heart to weep, as I thought of His wonderful love, in loving such a poor sinner as I was, and as I looked at Him, the devil's voice faded away, and at last I opened my heart, and lo! into it came such a wonderful peace and stillness. I thought no more, but just allowed Jesus to save me, and thus I passed from "death unto life," little realising at the time, nor even yet, indeed, the fulness of its meaning.

About a week after my conversion I was in my first prayer meeting, which consisted of about a dozen "well-saved sinners," and seeing they were willing to do what Jesus bade them—which means something—the devil told me straight they were too far on for me, and I ought to keep quiet for some months and not attract attention. God gave me grace there and then to resolve that I would wholly follow Him, or, in other words, be an out-and-out Christian. I praise God for this grace, as I now see that prayer meeting to have been a most critical time, and I also thank God because such a resolution places a soul above many of the petty temptations which beset the carnal Christian.

A few days after God took me at my word, and led me to destroy about £4 worth of pipes, and trust Him to take the desire away—as I was a hard smoker—and also to give me something in its place, and a better way of spending His money. In His unfailing bountiful way He responded to my faith, and I have never since had the least desire to smoke, which in itself is a great blessing in several ways as it proves to me if nothing else did, that my God is a living God.

Obeying what I believed to be the leading of God, I did not rush straight into whatever work presented itself, as it came to me that God had some work planned for me, and what I had to do was to allow Him to lead me into it ; and it seemed as if the Felt Street Interdenominational Mission Hall were to be the sphere. This was subsequently made plain to me as God's will. I have nothing whatever to say of my work here, as it was so utterly informal, but I found the work to be a joyful privilege, and every act to bear its own recompense in the sweet consciousness of realizing oneself to be a channel through which our great God and Father condescended to manifest His love and power to the needy souls in the district. God knows He was much and often straitened in me by the hindrances of self, but I do praise Him that He showed me at last my ugly "self" borne away by my Saviour, along with my sins on Calvary, and now I find that the Cross of Christ separates me from "myself" as well as my sins, so that being dead to self, the self-life no longer lives, but Christ (my New Life) liveth in me.

My conversion took place on the 15th of September, 1896, and about the following spring God was drawing out the hearts of some of my brothers in the Lord towards the heathen, and I felt very anxious to have a Missionary spirit, but God shewed me that it was His Gift, and was not to be found elsewhere or imitated, and so I received peace about it, and trusted Him to speak to me when His time came. At the same time He showed me I was not saved just to get to heaven, and that I must live for others, and tell out the news of the free grace of God. I believe He found me in some little way faithful in witnessing to those around me, for in July, at the Students' Conference in Curbar, I had the great joy of hearing Him say "I have need of you in Egypt." And so, after much waiting and prayer, I, with six other dear brothers, whom He has called to the same sphere, go forth in His glad service, being confident of this one thing, that He which hath begun, in and through me, a good work will perfect it until the day of Jesus Christ; for I know that in my flesh dwelleth no good thing, but I have been crucified with Christ: nevertheless I live; yet no longer I, but Christ liveth in me, and that life which I now live in the flesh, I live in faith, the faith which is in the Son of God Who loved me and gave Himself for me.

I pray you, dear reader, that you "quench not the Spirit," and abstain from every appearance of evil, and the God of peace Himself sanctify you wholly, and may your spirit and soul and body be preserved entire, without blame, at the coming of our Lord Jesus Christ.

"Faithful is He that calleth you, who also will do it."

JOHN GORDON LOGAN.

"*Ye shall receive the gift of the Holy Ghost.*
"*For the promise is unto you, and to your children, and to all that are afar off, even as many as the Lord our God shall call.*"
—ACTS ii. 38, 39.

"It was Thyself, O God, who sought,
With tender yearnings deep,
The loveless soul who sought Thee not,
The worthless, wandering sheep."

JOHN GORDON LOGAN.

FOR the first twenty years of my life I was dead to God, spiritually dead, and it was only after a terrible experience of shame and sin that my eyes were opened one day to see that Jesus had borne the sin-penalty, and my sin-sick, weary soul passed from death to life. I became alive to God, but, alas! very much alive to sin and self still. For three years He had to deal with me in a very stern way to wean my soul from the things of time and sense. I can well remember how it came at last to a whole-hearted surrender, a clean break with the world, and open confession of Christ at the street corner, and how the joy of the Lord flooded my soul. It meant death to sin, death to the world, and death to self, although there was very much I did not know anything about then. I surrendered up to my light, however, and when fresh light came never said "No" to my Lord. He began to use me in His service, filled me with a thirst for souls, and a love for His saints, but still there was something lacking. I felt a deep need of "power" in my life and service.

In July, 1891, the Lord drew very near. One afternoon I spent with a number of God's people in an upper room searching the Bible, prayerfully and diligently, regarding the Pentecostal Gift of the Holy Ghost. The Lord showed me clearly that there was such a gift. I could not look back to a time when I had definitely received, and my experience told me I was not in possession of this gift. The blessing was clearly for me (Acts ii. 17, 18, 38, 39) if I was willing to receive on God's terms; and as we knelt down I very humbly submitted myself wholly to God, to be and do whatever He required of me, and in simple faith received the Pentecostal Gift of the Holy Ghost, just as I had received the gift of eternal life some years before.

I knew but little that afternoon of what my risen, glorified Lord had done for me, I know but little now, for every day seems to bring fresh revelations of the presence and power of the Holy Ghost.

Shortly afterwards God tested to the uttermost the blessing I had received. A very clear call came to go to the heathen, to one of the darkest parts of Africa. To obey meant to be misunderstood and misjudged by loved ones, meant death to my home ties, to my friends, to every comfort, and facing a life of hardship and trial; but God brought me through more than conqueror, and when He saw I was willing to go all the way, He closed the door even more definitely than He had opened it. That was at the close of 1892, and for five years God sent me back to my business with one word to rest on— Rom. xi. 29, "The gifts and calling of God are without repentance."

During these years He began to reveal to me, as I was able to bear it, the utter corruption of the natural man. Especially did He open my eyes to see a subtle phase of the self-life I had never reckoned about. I refer to my beautiful, good, consecrated "self," with all its zeal for God's service, and its enjoyment of spiritual blessings, with its natural love, humility, joy, patience, generosity, wisdom, strength, and many other things, which I had not fully realised as being part of the old man, needing to be forever "devoted," given over to the death of the Cross. From that time everything seemed to go wrong. There was failure all along the line. I felt as if I had lost hold of God, and sometimes longed to be out of the work altogether. I could say with Job, "God hath overthrown me, and hath compassed me with His net; He hath stripped me of my glory, and taken the crown from my head." At the same time He began to send messages from various sources revealing to me the deeper meaning of the Cross, the Grave, the Resurrection and the Glory of Christ. The climax came one night, as I waited before God, and He made real to me experimentally, what I had long known in theory, that my own natural life came to an end with Christ's natural life on the Cross, and that it is "no longer I that live, but Christ liveth in me." Oh, how blind I had been! But from that night, "I, in the midst of life am daily delivered unto death for Jesus' sake, that the life whereby Jesus conquered death may show by faith its power in my dying flesh" (2 Cor. iv. 11. Conybeare's version). During the following night God confirmed what He had done—2 Cor. v. 14—17, especially "if any man be in Christ he is a new creature; old things are passed away; behold all things are become new." It has meant going down, down, deeper and deeper since, realizing every moment that "I am nothing" (2 Cor. xii. 11), that God is all, and that for every breath I must depend on Him alone.

During 1897 the impression became stronger and stronger that God was about to do a new thing in my experience. I had waited patiently in the very trying and difficult place He had put me in business, and had tested the faithfulness of El Shaddai to the utmost, not daring to step out of business until He called me. In October I was in Belfast, and met some of my dear brothers whom God had chosen for Egypt. They were praying for a seventh man to make up the band. I had no light about going to that country, and no desire on earth but for God and His will. Immediately after meeting them I received from the firm I was doing business for some samples of new goods, and, on looking them over, I saw at once it would be utterly impossible for me, as a follower of Jesus, to show them or receive profit from the sale of them. It would have grieved the Holy Ghost, and I felt in the depth of my being that all the wealth of the universe was but small dust in the balance compared with the smile of Jesus, and the joy of being well-pleasing unto Him. After taking the matter definitely to God for several days I wrote to the directors of the firm expressing my conviction, and, as there was no likelihood of the goods being withdrawn, resigning my situation. God gave me the twentieth verse of Psalm cxviii. (R. V.)—" This is the gate of the Lord, the righteous shall enter in "—as His message, and I felt He was about to take me out of business—but into what ?

It was coming very definitely to the souls of my Belfast brethren that God was answering their prayers for the seventh man, and taking me out for that purpose, and the impression deepened in my own mind that this was His will, and was confirmed on receiving a letter from the firm expressing their regret and accepting my resignation. Time and space would fail to tell how He has led on step by step, and how His voice was heard saying, "This is the way, walk ye in it," when the awful temptations and assaults of the enemy would have turned me to the right hand or the left. He made my parents and friends willing, nay glad, that I should go. "He hath broken the gates of brass, and cut the bars of iron in sunder !" Glory to His Name ! He gave me the blessed assurance that even should I never set foot in Egypt it has been gloriously worth while obeying Him in this matter. But never shall I forget how I looked to Him for some message from His Word to confirm it all, and, in a wonderful way, He gave me Genesis xlv. 18, 20—" Come unto me : and I will give you the good of the land of Egypt, and ye shall eat the fat of the land. Also regard not your stuff ; for all the good of the land of Egypt is yours."

GEORGE SWAN.

"O wretched man that I am! who shall deliver me from the body of this death? I thank God through Jesus Christ our Lord."—Rom. vii. 24, 25.

> "Thy beautiful sweet will, my God,
> Holds fast in its sublime embrace
> My captive will, a gladsome bird,
> Prisoned in such a realm of grace."

GEORGE SWAN.

ALTHOUGH not "born again" until 22 years of age, my spiritual history really dates back 11 years earlier, when at a large children's meeting, along with many others, I rose from my seat and went into the enquiry room. As far as I remember, my motive for doing so was more from a natural desire to be good than anything I heard in the address or any conviction of sin. My mind gripped nothing in the service nor in the personal dealing afterwards in the enquiry room, but simply with boy-like chivalry, I left that place determined to be "good," and set a good example to my brothers and sisters. Christ as a substitute for the penalty of sin, and a Saviour from the power of sin, was unknown to me. I only knew Him as an Example. To my surprise from that time I seemed to get worse and worse. As the days lengthened out into months, and the months into years, my experience was truly "for what I would, that do I not ; but what I hate, that do I," until the cry of my heart became, though at that time I could not have interpreted it, "Oh, wretched man that I am ! who shall deliver me from the body of this death ?" This struggle was entirely an internal one. Outwardly I was gay, happy, careless, and amongst moral people—moral, though the impurity of my heart poured forth its vileness in the presence of those who did not object to it. So deceptive was my life at this time that some of the most important offices of the church I attended were thrust upon me, under the delusion that I was a Christian. "Surely the heart of man is deceitful above all things and desperately wicked. Who shall know it ?"

About this time, when I was constantly dreading that the pent-up passions would break out into open sin, bringing ruin on myself and disgrace to my parents, I received a call to Ireland from a friend to consider a proposal to start business in Belfast. On arrival at my destination, a town in South-West Ulster, I found that I had to remain there over the week end, and on the Sunday went twice to church, but in the evening on coming out of church was asked by my friend's brother to go with him to a little mission hall in a poor part of the town. To this I gave a decided "No," and got out of his way as quickly as possible. When he returned to the house he asked why I so decidedly refused to go to the mission hall ? Upon which I opened out into a tirade against evangelicalism, mission work, and people who had the presumption to say they knew they were "saved." In reply to his question as to how I proposed to fit myself for the presence of God, and what was my plan of salvation, I said it was to add virtue to virtue, and grace to grace, setting myself to master one sin or evil habit at a time ; when that was got rid of to deal with another, and eventually trust to the clemency of God, that He would see I had done my best, and hence would *possibly* pass me at the judgment day. I must have had some vague idea of 2 Peter i. 6, 7, but knew nothing of verse 4, where it shows that one has to become a partaker of the "divine nature" before one can add to one's "faith virtue; and to virtue knowledge; and to knowledge temperance; and to temperance patience; and to patience godliness; and to godliness brotherly kindness; and to brotherly kindness love." From that evening my own argument as to the plan of salvation began to worry me, it being the first time I had ever stated it, and the first time I had ever been dealt with personally about my soul, and the very statement showed me what a refuge of lies I was hiding under, for I knew very well that I had been trying to live by that rule to the utmost of my ability for at least eleven years, and had only succeeded in adding vice to vice, and sin to sin. At the same time, although I told my friends I had met a religious fanatic, I could not forget his calm assurance.

After being at home for a fortnight I returned to Ireland to commence business in Belfast, and to my surprise within a few days I was introduced to one after another, who were of what I chose to call the fanatical type of Christian, namely, *who knew they were saved, and did not mind saying so.* On my first Sunday evening I was brought down to Felt Street Mission Hall. Everything was strange and wonderful. I had never been in such a place before. I began to see that the Lord's hand was upon me, and to look about to see what it was that He wanted to show me. Very gently He dealt with me, giving a little light here, and a little there, until eventually about the third Sunday night in Belfast, while praying a little child's prayer I had learnt at my mother's knee—"God bless father and mother, brothers and sisters, and make me a good boy"—when I got to the word "make," I realised how foolish I had been all these years, trying to "make" myself good, while all the time Jesus had died to do it for me. So I there and then cast the whole responsibility of my salvation on the Lord, and rose from my knees to notice for the first time the text over my bed, "Kept by the power of God," and from that time this has been my blessed experience, for I know Jesus not only as my Redeemer from the guilt and penalty of sin, but also as my Saviour from the power of sin.

DELIVERANCE AND TRANSLATION. 63

I cannot now look back upon the surroundings of my early Christian experience without the deepest thankfulness to God. I was associated with Felt Street Mission Hall from the first, and there it was that I tremblingly gave my first testimony. The healthy spiritual atmosphere of the place and scope for Christian activity, together with the fatherly care of the founder of the Mission, have had an influence in the moulding

WORK AMONGST HOME HEATHEN.

of my life which only eternity will reveal. Living and working in the locality revealed to me not only the awful havoc caused by sin, especially drunkenness, but the glorious power of the Gospel to raise the very lowest, and to meet every case of need. Looking back I can see now that God made Felt Street to be to me a Missionary College, and

I could not anywhere have had better training for the foreign field than I received during the four years of my connection with its work and workers.

About a month after my conversion I saw that the gift of the Holy Ghost, in His Pentecostal fulness, was mine for the taking, even as justification was; so I definitely, in faith, took God at His word and received the infilling of the Holy Ghost. Almost immediately God began to deal with me with regard to the heathen, and I was led to give myself to Him for the spread of the glad tidings to the Regions Beyond.

It was not until about a year after, in July, 1896, that I received further leading as to where the Lord wanted me to work, through a little pamphlet called a "A Challenge to Faith." This was a call for workers amongst Mohammedans, and the Lord showed this to be my sphere of labour for Him. About nine months after this, God began to call out a band of seven for the foreign field, and it was made clear to me that I was to be one of the number: and when a few months afterwards at the Students' Conference at Curbar, the call came for seven men for Egypt, it was manifest to me that this was of God, as it reconciled the individual leading to work among the Mohammedans with the leading of being one of the band of seven. And thus all along the line God has lovingly and gently led.

As I followed, the barred gates and blank walls gave way; the mountains were brought low, and the crooked places made straight.

All glory to His Name!

T. EDWARD SWAN.

"*Be still, and know that I am God: I will be exalted among the heathen, I will be exalted in the earth.*"—PSALM xlvi. 10.

> I heard the voice of Jesus say,
> "Come unto Me and rest;
> Lay down, thou weary one, lay down,
> Thy head upon My breast."

DELIVERANCE AND TRANSLATION.

I came to Jesus as I was—
  Weary, and worn, and sad;
I found in Him a resting-place,
  And He has made me glad.

I heard the voice of Jesus say,
  "Behold, I freely give
The living water—thirsty one,
  Stoop down, and drink, and live."
I came to Jesus, and I drank
  Of that life-giving stream;
My thirst was quenched, my soul revived,
  And now I live in Him.

I heard the voice of Jesus say,
  "I am this dark world's Light:
Look unto Me, thy morn shall rise,
  And all thy day be bright."
I looked to Jesus, and I found
  In Him my Star, my Sun;
And in that Light of Life I'll walk
  Till travelling days are done.

I WAS brought to a knowledge of the Lord Jesus Christ through attending a series of services held in Monaghan Parish Church by a saintly clergyman in January, 1889. Up to that time I had been an unsaved communicant in the Presbyterian Church, and went to it thinking that was the way I should get salvation. It was more than a month before I had assurance of salvation, and from about that time until April, 1897, I only knew what it was to be half saved. It was a case of "Oh, wretched man that I am! who shall

T. EDWARD SWAN.

deliver me?" and "when I would do good, evil was present with me;" and though I did not always succumb to temptation, it was often a desperate struggle to get the victory. I had not come to the end of myself for a full deliverance from sin, and though God blessed and owned my testimony for Him, still I did not know a Saviour Who was "able to save to the uttermost." Now, praise God, "He is my strength, and my song, and has also become my salvation." I do praise Him that I know a God that has saved me from having any sympathy with, love, or desire for sin. This great blessing was given me as I learned to sit before the Lord, and "be still" to know Him as God. Now, instead of praying as a duty or necessity, I find the greatest delight in waiting on God, and realize that He renews my spiritual and physical strength in a marvellous way, hitherto unknown to me. Praise God, I now find all my recreation in Christ Jesus. I know now what it is to "enjoy God."

Shortly after this full deliverance God shewed me I could not be absolutely surrendered to Him in the way He required me to be and remain at the particular work I was engaged in. Then through His Word, and in other ways, He began calling me to see His need in the foreign field; and, as I waited on Him for guidance, He clearly showed me I was to go forth in dependence on Him to Egypt. I had no hesitancy in obeying the call, but felt that not being much of a speaker this lack would probably be a hindrance. I found this a pretty hard difficulty to overcome, and at last God shewed me it was not the eloquence of the preacher or missionary that saved, but GOD IN THE MISSIONARY. Ultimately I obtained the victory, and became willing to be a contemptible vessel, that the excellency of the glory might be of God; and so I go forth realizing, as never before, that though I have nothing, yet I possess all things in Him, in Whom is all my sufficiency.

In the spring of 1896 I was at a Convention held in Enniskillen, and first became acquainted with two of the members of the present Egypt Mission Band; and, although only there for a day and a night, leaving at an early hour the following morning, a bond of love was formed that has grown stronger and stronger in Christ Jesus ever since. On my occasional visits to Belfast, after this, I generally made it a point of staying with one or other of these new found brothers in Christ, and joining them in seasons of waiting on God. On special occasions when God laid it on the heart of the Belfast Band to engage in some particularly aggressive work for Him, such as open-air campaigns on the event of public holidays and combined missions, I would unite with them. Though severed by a considerable distance, and with only very occasional meeting, God united us together in Him, and I always felt one with them. At the time when God had separated five out of the Band for foreign mission work, He laid my name on the hearts of every one of the five to pray that if it were the will of God I might be brought into line with His purpose.

No communication on the subject had been made up to this time, and no one outside of the five knew anything of the leading out to the foreign field. After they had begun to pray for me, I was led to write a letter (to one of them) to the effect that I realized that I had come to a crisis in my life, and that I could no longer wholly follow the Lord in my occupation, that I thought God was calling me to go to the Foreign Mission field trusting Him to supply my need. I was then invited down to spend Saturday to Monday with them in prayer and conference, where God confirmed to me the call for foreign service and the connection with the Band. At Curbar this call was again confirmed, and I there realized that I *must* go to Egypt if none of the others went. After my return home it was suggested that one of the number should take up work among the Jews. Before I received this communication, God had already laid the work upon my heart, and I was just writing away for information on the subject. With this confirmation of God's guidance, I felt myself in an especial manner separated unto the propagation of the Gospel amongst God's chosen people in Egypt.

ELIAS H. THOMPSON.

"Be careful for nothing; but in everything by prayer and supplication with thanksgiving let your requests be made known unto God. And the peace of God, which passeth all understanding, shall keep your hearts and minds through Christ Jesus."—PHIL. iv. 6, 7.

> Loved with everlasting love,
>   Led by grace that love to know;
> Spirit, breathing from above,
>   Thou hast taught me it is so!
> Oh, this full and perfect peace!
>   Oh, this transport all divine!
> In a love which cannot cease,
>   I am His, and He is mine.
>
> His for ever, only His;
>   Who the Lord and me shall part?
> Ah, with what a rest of bliss,
>   Christ can fill the loving heart!
> Heaven and earth may fade and flee,
>   Firstborn light in gloom decline,
> But, while God and I shall be,
>   I am His, and He is mine.

ELIAS H. THOMPSON.

I WAS brought up in a Christian home as a member of the Society of Friends, and from the earliest days of which I have any recollection have been kept in mind of the things of God. The first religious impressions that I remember came through a God-honoured evangelist when conducting a mission in Carrickfergus, and through a minister of our Society, who visited York while I was at school there. These, however, left but a very one-sided

DELIVERANCE AND TRANSLATION.

impression on my life, which might be summed up in the words "be good." An unsuccessful struggle began, and was carried on with an outward appearance of religion, whilst all the time the heart was far from God, and the desire for sin and the world ever present.

It was not till February, 1894, during a mission held in connection with the Presbyterian Congregation in White-abbey, by one of the Assembly's evangelists, that I first saw the Lord Jesus Christ crucified for me on the Cross of Calvary. The words of Ittai in 2 Samuel xv. 21 were adopted as the expression of my will. In life or death no king for me but Jesus. In looking back to that day I can see now that my attention was fixed more on the fact of my "determination" than the fact of His "reception," and for seven months I sought for "feeling," or outward testimony to the reality of the change that had taken place, till the Lord led me to see in simple faith that all our struggling is only our effort to "believe God," and when we believe Him we stop struggling and rest. It was then that Philippians iv. 6, 7, first came home to my soul. Through the reading of "Thoughts on Christian Sanctity," and some of the works of the Rev. Andrew Murray, the Lord showed me there was something more in His salvation than a deliverance from the guilt and penalty of sin, and I surrendered myself up to present light for all that the Lord willed for me. In the testing times, however, there was a drawing back, and therefore failure, and the consecration of the desire was rendered null by disobedience in action. Still the mercy and grace of the Lord led on, and the call came to me to leave business in the autumn of 1896, and go—"Not knowing whither." My eyes had been towards the Foreign Mission field, and, shortly after this last step, I attended a Conference of the Friends' Foreign Mission Association, in Darlington, hoping there to receive a call, but the Lord's time had not yet arrived; and from there I went to Rothesay to the Faith Mission Convention, where the Lord spoke to me very clearly on the fact of the necessity of union with Christ in His death if our lives are to bring forth fruit unto God.—John xii. 24.

Some work followed amongst the Society of Friends in the

South of Ireland, and still nothing definite opened before me, though the Lord was preparing His slowly yielding instrument for His work. My first connection with those with whom God was weaving in the thread of my life was in July, 1896, and from that time God began a blessed fellowship in the Holy Ghost. A five weeks' tour in the South of Ireland in the latter part of January and February, 1897, concluding with a series of meetings in Dublin, brought me into contact with one of the present band, who happened to be in Dublin at the time, and kindly took charge of the last meeting, specially convened for Christian workers, when many definitely received by faith the gift of the Holy Ghost.

On the occasion of the opening of the new Y.M.C.A. Buildings in Belfast, as I walked through the Minor Hall with a beloved evangelist, he said to me, "It is on my heart that the Lord is going to separate out a party from your band of thirteen for work in the Soudan." It was the first call to foreign work that came clearly home to my soul. The same "separation" was immediately laid on the hearts of two other brethren in the city, and became a subject of earnest prayer as to the Lord's will for us as individuals. The first idea that we had was that the Lord might send us to some untouched part of Southern Central Africa, which stands in so much need of the Gospel, but nothing came in that direction with the impress of Divine authority. Not being able to go to the Students' Conference at Curbar, as I was at Colwyn Bay for the Children's Special Services, the leading of the four who were there reached me by letter. I found it necessary to come home for a Sunday, and then met the brethren for united prayer. Before going to bed on Sunday night, 22nd of August, 1897, I asked the Lord to give a message from His Word as to whether He wanted me to go to Egypt, and when I opened the Bible it seemed to contain Egypt on every page I turned to. Next morning before going to meet one of the brethren, the word came from Ezekiel x. 22—"They went every one straight forward," which proved to be the very word this brother had received as a message to the band.

Again on Sunday, 26th September, as we unitedly waited on the Lord He spoke very definitely to me, and I saw there was

DELIVERANCE AND TRANSLATION.

nothing for me to do but let the Lord have His way, though I had not yet the spiritual assurance, apart from the written Word, of God's purpose on my behalf. Shortly after this the Lord led me to visit my brother in the South of France, when He spoke to me very definitely through two of His servants, revealing the subtleties of the self-life, and the need of the experimental out-working of much that had formerly been held theoretically or intellectually.

He dealt on the negative side through the sparing of the Amalekites by Saul in 1 Samuel xv., and on the positive side through the history of King Asa, especially in 2 Chronicles xvi. 9—the need of a perfect heart before God which He alone could give. Then all seemed dark for some days, but the promises of Malachi iii. 1-3 and iv. 1-3 were given to me and I waited their fulfilment.

The next step was to be sent with a friend who was going to conduct some meetings with the Missionaries in Algiers, and there in one of the Missionaries' homes, face-to-face with a few native converts, the Lord fulfilled His promises. As I left the room, the word sounded in my inward ear, "The days of Thy mourning are ended." Hallelujah! At the same time He set His seal to the call to carry to the Gentiles the "unsearchable riches of Christ." One by one the doors opened, and on the 17th of January, 1898, the shores of England were left behind, a parting shot being fired to the few labourers standing on the quay wall as we emerged into the Mersey—" The wages of sin is death, but the gift of God is eternal life through Jesus Christ our Lord."

To Him be all the glory. Amen.

THE SPHINX AT GHIZEH, NEAR CAIRO.

CHAPTER V.

The Land and its People.

Arise and work ! arise and pray
That He would haste the dawning day !
And let the silver trumpet sound
Wherever Satan's slaves are found.

The vanquished foe shall soon be stilled,
The conquering Saviour's joy fulfilled,
Fulfilled in us, fulfilled in them,
His crown, His royal diadem.

Soon, soon our waiting eyes shall see
The Saviour's mighty jubilee !
His harvest joy is filling fast,
He shall be satisfied at last.

Condition of the Country. ALTHOUGH some accounts of the Classics may be deemed exaggerated when they speak of the population and prosperity of Egypt, we cannot accuse them of error, except in the number of towns and inhabitants of the country ; for the monuments show us how rich was Egypt under the native rulers, and indicate to what cause this may reasonably be assigned. From the time at which the great Pyramid was built, to the Persian invasion, a period of between 2,000 and 3,000 years, the population of Egypt and its extent of cultivated land far exceeded what they are in the present day. The country does not seem to have been over-peopled. Many causes tended to prevent this, particularly serious wars in which the Pharaohs engaged. The long and desolating struggles with the Assyrians and Persians inflicted a severe blow on the interests of the country. Under the

Macedonians it recovered much of its former prosperity; and when the Romans held Egypt it was one of their most productive provinces, and the granary of the Empire. During the Roman rule various political causes contributed to the decline of the population. After the Moslem conquest this decay continued, almost uninterruptedly, until the time of the Fatimees; but from that until the Turkish conquest the rulers of the successive independent dynasties generally governed the country with a regard for its interests, and cannot be accused of the systematic tyranny and misrule of the Turkish Pashas. There was a temporary recovery under the independent or semi-independent Memlock rulers before the French invasion, and in spite of much of the Turkish system the country has again made good progress. But it is since the English occupation that Egypt has taken a new lease of life; and with a continuation of good Government we may trust that the future has happier days in store for the country.

Agriculture. Under the Pharaohs Egypt was an agricultural country, and both commerce and manufacture were unimportant. The main energies of the people were expended in turning to the best account soil of unexcelled richness, annually watered and renewed by the river Nile. This natural policy was the true one for the prosperity of the country. From the sculptures and paintings of the tombs we form a clear idea of the agriculture of the ancient Egyptians, while the classical writers give us information respecting the tenure of lands and the laws for the cultivator.

Origin and Present Conditions of the Egyptians. For thousands of years the banks of the Nile have been occupied by the Egyptians, the oldest nation known to history, and still exhibiting many of their ancient personal characteristics unaltered. Notwithstanding the interminable series of immigrations and other changes affecting the character of the inhabitants, the Egyptian type has always predominated with marvellous uniformity. As Egypt is said to be "the gift of the Nile," so has the character of its inhabitants been apparently moulded

A DAY OF CALM ON THE RIVER NILE.

by the influence of that river. No country in the world is so dependent on a river which traverses it as Egypt, and no river presents physical characteristics so exceptional as the Nile; so, too, there exists no race of people which possesses so marked and unchanging an individuality as the Egyptians. It is, therefore, most probable that this unvarying type is the product of the soil itself, and that the character of the peoples who settled at different periods on the banks of the Nile, whatever it may originally have been, has in due course of time been moulded to the same constant form by the mysterious influences of the river. In all countries, indeed, national characteristics are justly regarded as the outcome of soil and climate, and of this connection no country affords so strong an illustration as Egypt, with its sharply defined boundaries of sea and desert, and in its complete isolation from the rest of the world. These considerations tend to throw serious doubts on all current theories as to the origin of the Egyptians. According to the Bible, Mizraim was the son of Ham, and brother of Canaan and the Ethiopian Cush; and as his name was applied by the Hebrews to Egypt, it is probable that he migrated with his sons from Asia to the banks of the Nile. The name, moreover, of Ludim, his eldest son, corresponds to the word Rotu, or Lotu, the hieroglyphic name for the Egyptians.

Philologists, who have discovered points of resemblance in the roots and inflections of the ancient Egyptian and Semitic languages, likewise come to the conclusion that the Egyptians originally came from Asia, either by way of Suez or across the Red Sea from Arabia.

The Modern Egyptians.

The population of Egypt, according to the census returns of 1897, is composed as follows:—

Arabs	8,399,309
Copts	608,446
Bedouins	573,974
Ottoman subjects (including some Syrians and Greeks)	40,150
Foreigners	112,526
Total	9,734,405

The Land and its People.

Divided in Lower Egypt	...	5,676,109
,, ,, Upper Egypt	...	4,058,296

And the divisions according to Religions are mainly composed of:—

Mohammedans	... ...	8,978,775
Christians (Greeks, Catholics, etc.)	...	730,162
Jews	... ...	25,200
Others (Idol Worshippers)	...	268
Total	... ...	9,734,405

Men—4,947,850; 1½ per cent. read and write, say 436,000 altogether.

Women—4,786,555; 6 per thousand read and write, say 32,000 altogether.

Nearly all the Egyptian women who can read and write have belonged to the American Mission, and are Copts.

* * *

The inhabitants may be divided between the following different classes :—

(1.) THE FELLAHIN, "the tillers" or "peasants," form the bulk of the population, and may be regarded as the sinews of the national strength. They are generally slightly above the middle height; their bones, and particularly their skulls, are strong and massive; and their wrists and ankles are powerful and somewhat clumsy. In all these respects the fellahin, as well as their domestic animals, contrast strongly with the inhabitants of the desert. Notwithstanding this largeness of frame, however, the fellah never grows fat. The women and girls are particularly remarkable for their slender build, and they often speak of each other as *zei el-habl*, or slender as a rope. The men generally keep their heads shaved, but the hair of the soldiers and the long tresses of the girls, though always black and often curly, is by no means of the short woolly negro type.

The dwelling of the fellah is of a miserably poor description, consisting generally of four low walls formed of crude bricks of Nile mud, and thatched with a roof of dura straw, rush, rags, or old straw mats. In the interior are a few mats, a sheep's skin, several baskets made of matting, a copper kettle, and a few earthenware pots and wooden dishes. Instead of using the crude bricks, the fellahin in Upper Egypt often form

A MOHAMMEDAN WOMAN.

the walls of their huts of a mixture of mud and straw. The dark, windowless interior is entered by a small opening, in front of which the proprietor usually forms an enclosure of circular shape with a wall of mud about five feet in height.

This is the court-yard of the establishment, and the usual resort of the family and their domestic animals in summer. The walls of the yard generally contain round hollows, used as receptacles for the grain which forms the food of the family. Within the yard are usually placed a square pillar, about five feet in height, with openings in its sides, as receptacles for objects of value, and a thick column of the same height terminating in a platform, shaped like a plate, with the edges bent upwards, which is used by the proprietor as a sleeping-place in hot weather. The fact is that beneath an Egyptian sky, houses are not of the same paramount importance as in more northern regions, all that is wanted being shelter for the night.

The poorer peasant's mode of life is frugal in the extreme. The staple of his food consists of a peculiar kind of bread made of sorghum flour in Upper Egypt, or of maize in the Delta, wheaten bread being eaten by the wealthier only. This poor kind of bread often has a greenish colour owing to an admixture of bean-flour. Next in importance in the bill of fare are broad beans. For supper, however, even the poorest cause a hot repast to be prepared. This usually consists of a highly-salted sauce made of onions and butter, or in the poorer houses of onions and linseed or sesame oil. Into this sauce, which in summer acquires a gelatinous consistency by the addition of the universal bamia and various herbs, each member of the family dips pieces of bread held in the fingers. Both in town and country goats', sheeps', or buffaloes' milk also forms a daily article of food, but always in a sour condition or half converted into cheese, and in very moderate quantities only. In the height of summer the consumption of fruit of the cucumber and pumpkin series, which the land yields in abundance, is enormous. In the month of Ramadan alone, when a rigorous fast is observed during the day, and on the three days of the great Beiram festival, even the poorest members of the community indulge in meat, and it is customary to distribute that rare luxury to beggars at these seasons.

The agricultural population of Egypt is only about two

millions, an unnaturally low population when we consider the character of the country. The sole wealth of Egypt is

AN ARAB WATER-CARRIER.

derived from its agriculture, and to the fellahin alone is committed the important task of tilling the soil. They are, indeed, neither fitted nor inclined for other work, a circumstance which proves how completely the stationary character of the ancient Egyptians has predominated over the restless Arabian blood, which has been largely infused into the native population ever since the valley of the Nile was conquered by the armies of El-Islam. The modern Egyptians, moreover, resemble the ancient in the lot to which they are condemned. In ancient times the fellah, pressed into the service of the priests and the princes, was compelled to yield up to them the fruits of his toil, and his position was nearly the same to the present day, save that the names of his masters were changed, until relief came owing to the almost entire abolition of compulsory work since the British occupation.

In his own fields the fellah is an industrious labourer, and his work is more continuous than that of the peasant of more northern countries. He enjoys no period of repose during the winter, and the whole of his spare time is occupied in drawing water for the irrigation of the land. Notwithstanding his hard lot, however, he is an entire stranger to any endeavour to better his condition or to improve his system of farming. As soon as he has accomplished the most necessary tasks he rests and smokes, and trusts that Allah will do the remainder of his work for him.

The fellah is a believer in the religion of Mohammed, although he knows but little of the prophet's doctrine and history. Followers of all other religions he believes to be doomed to eternal perdition; but travellers are not on that account disliked by him. They serve rather to confirm his belief in eternal justice, for he is convinced that all the comforts and luxuries they now enjoy will be counterbalanced by torments hereafter. At the same time he admires and over-rates our knowledge, which is so superior to his own. Every well-dressed European is, in the estimation of the natives, a prodigy of wisdom; and, as their ideas of a scholar and a physician are identical, they place implicit reliance on our ability to heal the sick and save the dying. The traveller who comes in contact with the fellahin will often be applied to for medicine, and will find drugs more effective than money in securing their goodwill.

(2.) COPTS.—While we have regarded the fellahin as genuine Egyptians in consequence of their uninterrupted occupation of the soil, the religion of the Copts affords us an additional guarantee for the purity of their descent. The Copts are undoubtedly the most direct descendants of the ancient Egyptians, there being no ground for the assumption that their ancestors were foreign immigrants who embraced Christianity after the conquest of the country by the Mohammedans; while on the other hand the obstinacy with which they defended their monophysite Christianity for several centuries against the inroad of the creed of Byzantium affords another indication of their Egyptian character. The Coptic population is officially stated as over half a million, *i.e.*, about a fifth of the purely indigenous population of the valley of the Nile. They are most numerous in the towns of Northern Egypt, around the ancient Coptos, at Negada, Luksor, Esneh, Dendera, Girgeh, Tahta, and particularly at Siut and Akhmim. A large proportion of the population of all these places is Coptic.

Most of the Copts are dwellers in towns, and are chiefly engaged in the more refined handicrafts as watchmakers, goldsmiths, jewellers, embroiderers, tailors, weavers, manufacturers of spurious antiquities, etc.; or in trade, or as clerks, accountants, and notaries. Their physique is accordingly materially different from that of the fellahin. They are generally somewhat below the middle height, and of delicate frame, with small hands and feet. Their skulls are higher and narrower than those of the peasantry, and with less protruding cheek bones, and their complexion is fairer. These differences are sufficiently accounted for by their mode of life; for when we compare those Copts who are engaged in rustic pursuits, or the Coptic camel drivers of Upper Egypt, with the fellahin, we find that the two races are not distinguishable from each other.

Few nations of the East embraced the Gospel more zealously than the dwellers on the Nile. Accustomed as they had long been to regard life as a pilgrimage to death, as a school of preparation for another world, and weary of their motley and confused Pantheon of divinities, whose self-seeking priesthood designedly disguised the truth, they eagerly welcomed the simple doctrines of Christianity, which appeared so well adapted to their condition, and promised them succour and redemption. Like Eutyches, they revered the divine nature of the Saviour only, in which they held that every human element was absorbed ; and when the Council of Chalcedon in 451 sanctioned the doctrine that Christ combined a human with a divine nature, the Egyptians with their characteristic tenacity, adhered to their old views, and formed a sect termed Eutychians or Monophysites, to which the Copts of the present day still belong.

The traveller may distinguish the Copts from the Arabs by their dark turbans, which are generally blue or black, and their dark coloured clothes. This costume was originally prescribed by their oppressors, and they still take a pride in it as mark of their origin, though now permitted to dress as they please. A practised eye will also frequently detect among them the ancient Egyptian cast of features. Towards strangers the Copt is externally obliging, and when anxious to secure their favour he not unfrequently appeals to his Christian creed as a bond of union. Many Copts have recently been converted to Protestantism through the American Mission, particularly in Upper Egypt, chiefly by the good schools and the distribution of cheap Arabic Bibles. Even the orthodox Copts have a great reverence for the sacred volume, and it is not uncommon to meet with members of their sect who know the whole Gospels by heart.

(3.) **BEDUINS.**—" Bedu " is the name applied to the nomadic Arabs, and " Arab " to those who immigrated at a later period and settled in the valley of the Nile. They both differ materially from the dwellers in towns, and from the fellahin, who usually call themselves " Sons of the Arabs."

The Beduins may be divided into two leading groups—(1.) Beduins in the narrower sense, *i.e.*, Arabic-speaking tribes, most of whom have probably immigrated from Arabia or Syria, and who occupy the deserts adjoining Central and Northern Egypt, or who are to be found in different regions of Southern Nubia as a pastoral people ; (2.) " Bega," who range over the regions of Upper Egypt and Nubia, situated between the Nile and the Red Sea, and extending to the frontiers of the Abyssinian mountains, their territory being known as "Edbai." To these last the name of Ethiopians may as accurately be applied as that of Arabs to the first group, and they are believed by Dr. Lepsius to be the descendants of the Blemmyes, who occupied the Nubian part of the valley of the Nile down to the fourth century after Christ, when they were expelled by the "Nubian" invaders from the south. The second group consists of three different races—the Hadendoa, the Bisharin, and the Ababdeh. The last-named, who are widely scattered in the valleys of the desert between the tropics of Keneh and Koser, and who lead a poverty-stricken life with their very scanty stock of camels and goats are those with whom we have alone to deal as inhabitants of Egypt. Though closely resembling the other Bega tribes in appearance, the Ababdeh possess an original language of their own, which, however, they have long since exchanged for bad Arabic. Besides the girdle round their loins they wear a kind of long, white shirt, and in winter a light-coloured striped woollen mantle, while the Bisharin and Hadendoa tend their large flocks of sheep and herds of camel in a half naked condition, with a leathern apron, and wrapped in a kind of blanket.

They are nominally Mohammedans, but they do not pray or keep the fast of Ramadan, or make pilgrimages, except on rare occasions.

The Beduins of the North have inherited with comparative purity the fiery blood of the desert tribes, who achieved such marvellous exploits under the banner of the Prophet, but the traveller will rarely come in contact with them unless he undertakes a journey across the desert. The loiterers who assist travellers in the ascent of the Pyramids and pester them to buy antiquities, which are generally spurious, call themselves Beduins; but, even if originally of that race, they have entirely lost all its nobler characteristics in consequence of their intercourse with strangers and their debasing occupations. Genuine Beduins are to be found nowhere except in their desert home, where to a great extent they still retain the spirit of independence, the courage and the restlessness of their ancestors. As in the time of Herodotus, the tent of the Beduin is still his home. Where it is pitched is a matter of indifference to him, if only the pegs which secure it be firmly driven into the earth, if it shelter his wife and child from the burning sunshine and the chilly night air, and if pasturage ground and a spring be within reach.

In consequence of the frequent wars waged between the different tribes every Beduin is a warrior.

(4.) ARAB DWELLERS IN TOWNS.—Those Arabs with whom the traveller usually comes in contact in towns are shopkeepers, officials, servants, coachmen, and donkey-attendants, or perhaps these last only, as most of the best shops are kept by Europeans, while in official and legal matters his intercourse with the natives is carried on through the medium of his consul. The indolence and duplicity of these Arabs, which proceed to some extent from the character of their religion, have often been justly condemned, while their intelligence, patience, and amiability are too often ignored. They are generally of a much more mixed origin than the fellahin, as the various conquerors of Egypt usually made the towns their headquarters. Alexandria, for example, was chiefly favoured by the Greeks and Arabs, and Cairo by the Arabs and Turks. It thus happens that the citizens of the Egyptian towns consist of persons of every complexion, from dark brown to white, with the features of the worshippers of Osiris, or the sharp profile of the Beduins, and with the slender figure of the fellah or the corpulence of the Turk. Among the lower classes frequent intermarriage with negro women has darkened the complexion and thickened the features of their offspring; while the higher ranks, being descended from the white slaves or Turkish mothers, more nearly resemble the European type.

A glance at the offices of the ministers, the bazaars of the merchants, the schools of the Arabs, and the building yards and workshops constructed by the natives, will enable the traveller to observe with what deliberation and what numerous intervals of repose they perform their tasks. From such workers it is vain to expect rapidity, punctuality, or work of a highly-finished character.

NUBIANS.

(5.) BERBERS.—The name "Berberi" is believed by many authorities to be identical with "barbarians," a word which is said to have been adopted by the Greeks from the Egyptians, who used it to denote all "non-Egyptians," and to be derived from brr, *i.e.*, "to be unable to speak," or "to speak imperfectly." The Berbers of North Africa and the town of Berber in South Nubia also doubtless have the same origin. In Egypt the name is applied in a half contemptuous way to the numerous immigrants from the Nubian part of the valley of the Nile, who form the largest foreign element of the community, and who never entirely assimilate with it, as the Nubians make it a rule never to marry Egyptian wives.

The Nubians are inferior to the Egyptians in industry and energy, and especially in tilling the soil, and also in physical strength, and they are more superstitious and fanatical, as is indicated by the numerous amulets they wear round their necks and arms. They are, however, superior to the Egyptians in cleanliness, honesty, and subordination, and possess a more highly developed sense of honour.

In their native country they till the banks of the Nile, but their land is of very limited extent and poorly cultivated; and as their harvests are scanty, they are rarely able to support large families. They accordingly often immigrate at an early age to the richer lowlands, chiefly to the large towns, and particularly to Alexandria, in quest of employment; and they find no difficulty in attaining their object, for they are generally active, intelligent, and honest, while the older immigrants, who are strongly attached to their country, are always zealous in procuring them work and rendering them assistance. When the Berber has succeeded in amassing a moderate fortune he returns to settle in his native country, of which throughout his whole career he never entirely loses sight, and to which he frequently remits his hard-earned savings for the benefit of his relations. The cold winter nights in Egypt are very trying to the poor Berbers, who often have to sleep in the open air, outside the doors, and many of them are attacked by consumption.

(6.) NEGROES.—Like the Berbers, most of the negroes in Egypt are professors of El-Islam, to the doctrines of which they readily and zealously attach themselves. Most of the older negroes and negresses with whom the traveller meets have originally been brought to Egypt as slaves, and belong to natives, by whom they are treated more like members of the family than like servants. Although every slave who desires to be emancipated may now, with the aid of Government, sever the ties which bind him to his master, most of the negroes prefer to remain on the old footing with the family which supports them, and relieves them of the anxiety of providing for themselves.

(7.) **TURKS.**—Although the dynasty of the viceroys of Egypt is of Turkish origin a comparatively small section of the community belongs to that nation, and their numbers appear to be diminishing. The Turks of Egypt are chiefly to be found in the towns, where most of them are Government officials, soldiers, and merchants. The Turkish officials are responsible for the maladministration which so long paralysed the rich productiveness of the Valley of the Nile, having always, with few exceptions, been actuated in their proceedings by motives of reckless cupidity, without regard to ulterior consequences.

(8.) **LEVANTINES.**—A link between the various classes of dwellers in Egypt and the visitors to the banks of the Nile is formed by the various Mediterranean races known as Levantines, who have been settled here for several generations, and form no inconsiderable element in the populations of the larger towns. Most of them profess the Latin form of Christianity, and Arabic has now become their mother tongue, although they still speak their old national dialects. They are apt linguists, learning the European languages with great rapidity, and good men of business, and owing to these qualities are often employed as shopmen and clerks.

(9.) **ARMENIANS AND JEWS.**—This section of the community is about as numerous as the last, and in some respects contrasts favourably with it. The Armenians generally possess excellent abilities, and a singular aptitude for learning both Oriental and European languages, which they often acquire with great grammatical accuracy. Many of them are wealthy goldsmiths and jewellers, and they often hold important Government offices.

The Jews are often distinguishable by their red hair from the native Egyptians, as well as by other characteristics. Most of them are from Palestine, but many have recently immigrated from Wallachia. All the money-changers in the streets and many of the wealthiest merchants of Egypt, are Jews, and notwithstanding the popular prejudice entertained against them, owing as is alleged to their disregard of cleanliness, they now form one of the most highly-respected sections of the community.

(10.) **EUROPEANS.**—The number of European residents and visitors in Egypt is about 110,000, exclusive of the British army of occupation. The Greeks are most numerously represented, then the Italians, French, English (including Maltese), Austrians (including many Dalmatians), and Germans. The numerous Swiss residents in Egypt, who are not represented by a Consul of their own, are distributed among the above leading classes—French, Italian, and German. Beside these nationalities, there are also a few representatives of Russia, America, Belgium, Scandinavia, and other countries. Each of the above leading nationalities shows a preference for one or more particular occupations in which they enjoy a complete monopoly. The Greeks of all classes are generally traders. They constitute the aristocracy of Alexandria, and the provision dealers in all other towns are mostly Greeks.

With regard to the capability of Europeans becoming acclimatised in Egypt, there are a number of widely divergent opinions. Each, of course, must depend on the nature of the climate of their own respective countries. It has been asserted that European families, settled in Egypt, die out in the second or third generation, but of this there is no sufficient proof, as the European community is of very recent origin, and many examples to the contrary might be cited. The climate of Egypt is less enervating than that of most other hot countries, an advantage attributed to the dryness of the air, and the saline particles contained in it; while the range of temperature between the different seasons is greater than in Ireland or Portugal.

To turn to the land itself the first sight is by no means prepossessing, for the northern coast is low and barren, presenting no view of interest, and affording no indication of the character of the country which it bounds. It is a barrier generally of sandhills, but sometimes a rock juts out, for the most part wholly destitute of vegetation except where a few wild and stunted date palms grow.

Immediately behind are desolate marsh tracts or extensive salt lakes, and beyond these the fertile country.

The last is a wide plain intersected by two branches of the Nile and by many canals, of which some were anciently branches of the river, and having a soil of great richness, though in this particular it is excelled by the valley above. The only inequalities of the surface are the mounds of ancient towns, and on these, if not always ancient, stand the modern towns and villages. The palm trees are less numerous and not so beautiful as in the more southern part of the country, but other trees are more common. The houses and huts of the towns and villages are of burnt bricks near the Mediterranean, but as the climate becomes drier and the occurrence of rain less frequent the use of crude bricks obtain, until near the point of the Delta it is very general.

The towns of the northern coast, the most western Alexandria, called by the natives El-Iskendereeyh, is the largest and most important. It was founded in the year B.C. 332 by Alexander the Great, who gave it the form of a Macedonian mantle. The ancient city occupied the space between the sea and Lake Mareotis, being about four miles in its greatest length and a little less than a mile in its greatest breadth. The island of Pharos was likewise inhabited, and was joined to the Continent by the mole called Heptastidium. The Heptastidium and the island divided the Bay into two harbours. These were spacious, and, although the western, anciently called Portus Eunosti, but now the old port, is difficult to enter, and the eastern Magnus Portus, or the new port, is not so deep and less secure, they are, except Port Said, by far the best anchorages on this coast of Egypt.

The older part of the town of Alexandria stands upon a Heptastidium now much wider than it was anciently; but the

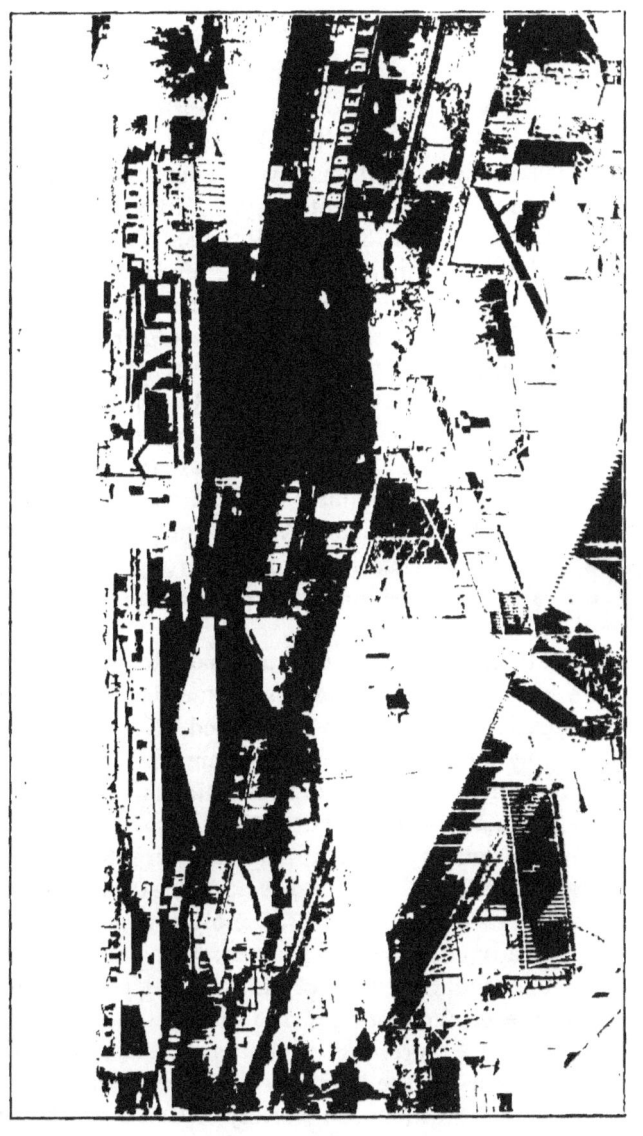

PORT SAID.

recent part, where are the houses of the European merchants, occupies the site of a portion of the ancient city which was nearest the mole. The most striking is a castle on the island of Pharos, containing a lighthouse which has succeeded to the more famous Pharos of antiquity. Here also is the Khedive's palace, as well as the lesser Pharos. The houses of the towns are built of stone, or have their lower storey cased with that material and the portion built of brick plastered and whitewashed. The residences of the European merchants and consuls, and the richer Turks and natives, are spacious and well built, somewhat in the modern Italian style, but have no claims to architectural beauty. The mosques are not remarkable, but the English church will be a great ornament to the town. The population of the town is estimated at over 200,000. One of the favourite projects of Mehemet Ali was the fortification of Alexandria, it has been thus rendered so strong that if well garrisoned it is said it could not be invested by a force of less than about 40,000 men.

Cairo is still the most remarkable and characteristic of Arab cities. The beauty of its religious and domestic architecture, before the recent innovations is unexcelled elsewhere. The edifices raised by the Moorish kings of Spain, and the Moslem rulers of India, may have been more splendid in their materials and more elaborate in their details; the houses of the great men of Damascus may be more costly than were those of the Memlock Beys, but for purity of choice and elegance of design both are far excelled by many of the mosques and houses in Cairo. These mosques have suffered much in the beauty of their appearance from the effects of time and neglect, but their colour has been even thus softened and their outlines rendered more beautiful and picturesque. What is most to be admired in their style of architecture is its extraordinary freedom from restraint, shown in the wonderful variety of its forms and the skill in design which has made the most intricate details harmonious with grand outlines. Here the student may best learn the history of Arab art.

CHAPTER VI.

The Pre-eminence of Prayer in connection with Missions, and our Duty towards Egypt.

"*Continue steadfastly in prayer.*"—COL. iv. 2 (R.V.).

"*Brethren, pray for us, that the Word of the Lord may run and be glorified, . . .*"—2 THESS. iii. 1 (R.V.).

> Keep on sowing—
> God will cause the seeds to grow
> Faster than your knowing.
> Nothing e'er is sown in vain,
> If, His voice obeying,
> You look upward for the rain,
> And falter not in praying.
>
> Keep on praying—
> In the brightest, darkest day,
> Still His voice obeying;
> Never from the gates of prayer
> Turn with doubting sorrow,
> For the One who standeth there
> May answer you to-morrow.

THROUGHOUT the whole missionary world there is at present a great sense of need. In every report of every society this finds expression; in every letter of every missionary this is revealed. Opposed as our missionaries are by the gigantic and growing masses of heathenism, they feel overwhelmingly their own helplessness. The power of evil is so terrific, and the forces of evil are so active, that they are apt to despair. So from every land the cry of the Missionaries comes to our ears. And what do they cry for? Not men; not money; but prayer. Above even the urgent cry, "Come over and help us" (and God knows they have enough cause to utter that cry) we can hear the words, "Brethren, pray for us."

In this deepened sense of the need of prayer, which is noticeable on every side, we have a token that the Church is entering into fuller sympathy with her Lord. For the Lord Jesus has all along told us that the supreme need of missionary work is prayer. In His first utterance on the question He made this plain: "When He saw the multitudes He was moved with compassion because they fainted, and were scattered abroad as sheep having no shepherd. Then saith He unto His disciples 'The harvest truly is plenteous, but the labourers are few. Pray ye, therefore.'"

Before "Give," before "Go," comes "Pray." This is the Divine order, and any attempt to alter it will end in disaster. Prayer is to missionary work what air is to the body, the element in which it lives. Missions were born in prayer, and can only live in an atmosphere of prayer. *The very first duty of a Church in organising its Foreign Missionary work is to awaken, maintain, and sustain in its members the spirit of prayer.*

Some reasons may now be given why this pre-eminent place should be assigned to prayer :—

1. Prayer keeps us continually in mind of what the true basis and the true character of missionary work is. He who prays never forgets that the work is God's. Prayer puts God first. It reminds us that He is the supreme worker. It reminds us that He is the supreme director. It reminds us, also, that only in so far as we follow the line of His will can we hope for true success; and it inclines us to wait on God, that He may reveal His will to us. How important all this is, especially to our Missionary Committees and Boards, it is needless to state. He who prays will have his heart brought more and more into sympathy with God's purpose, and ever be ready to do God's work in God's way.

2. Prayer supplies the means by which the needs of our missionary work may be met. The first great need of missions is men. If the harvest field is to be reaped, we must have labourers. But how are these labourers to be got? Surely by prayer. Is not this what the Lord told us—"Pray ye, therefore, the Lord of the harvest that He will send labourers into His harvest." The shortest way to get Missionaries is the way that leads by the throne of God. Appeals to God will man the fields more quickly and more efficiently than appeals to man. *In the evangelization of the world the missionary prayer meeting is a greater force than the missionary public meeting. A praying Church never lacks Missionaries.* If Missionaries are not forthcoming to carry on the Church's work, it is a sure sign that that work has not the place it ought to have in the Church's prayers.

The second great need of missions is money. The Apostle puts the two together when he says, "How shall they hear without a preacher? and how shall they preach except they be sent?" Money is needed. How is it to be obtained? By prayer. The silver and the gold belong to the Lord, and, in answer to believing prayer, He can bring it forth from the purses and pockets of His people. This we have to learn. Teach people to pray, and you have taught them to give. People will always give for the support of a work which has a real place in their prayers. If our Missionary Committees and Boards were only half as anxious about having the prayers of our people as about having their gifts; if they took as much pains to stimulate prayer as they take to stimulate giving, our missionary treasuries would be full to overflowing.

3. Prayer meets needs in connection with our missionary work which can be met in no other way. This is a matter of the utmost importance. If we realised how much has to be done in connection with missions which can only be done by prayer, we should realise the urgency of the question.

We appoint a committee or a board to manage our missionary work. But how shall we secure that it will act wisely, or rightly employ the means put at its disposal? Only by prayer. We invite men to be our representatives in the foreign field. How shall we secure that the right men come forward? Only by prayer. We send these men into the heathen field. How shall we preserve them against discouragement, against faintheartedness, against unbelief, against laziness? Only by prayer. Nothing else will do it. The best men that can be obtained for such service need to be continually upheld. *A Church has no right to send out any man unless she is prepared to uphold him by prayer.*

We gather out from among the heathen, by the work of our Missionaries, groups of men and women, and bring them into the fellowship of the Christian Church. How are we to encourage them, and keep them true? Only by prayer. Here is a girl who has been trained in one of our mission schools. She has given her heart to Christ, and has been a great joy to her teacher. But she is taken by her parents, who are still heathen, given in marriage to a heathen man, and sent away to live in a heathen village. How are we to comfort and uphold that girl? Our Missionaries cannot do it. They are not where she is. Our money cannot do it. It is not money she wants. Our prayers, and our prayers alone can do it. Needs like these can be met in no other way. The fact is, prayer is an absolute necessity for the proper carrying on of missionary work. If it is to prosper it must be steeped in prayer.

But something must now be said as to the character of the prayer which is needed for missionary work. It must be prayer that costs us something.

(*a*)—**Prayer for Missions must be Intelligent.**

Many pray for missions whose prayers are practically valueless because of their ignorance. How can a man's prayers be supposed to be real if he will not take the trouble to inform himself about that for which he pretends to pray. Missionary prayer burns hotly only when fed with the fuel of missionary information. Prayer must be based on knowledge. And the knowledge which leads to true missionary prayer is two-fold:

(1). It is a knowledge of the principles of missions, that is, *a knowledge of what God wishes to be done.* This can only be obtained by honest, prayerful, long-continued study of God's Word. There God's will is revealed. What it is we must discover, for we cannot pray aright for missions who will not take pains to discover God's thoughts about them.

(2). It is a knowledge of missionary facts, that is, *a knowledge of what God is actually doing*. This can only be obtained by painstaking study of missionary literature and diligent attendance at missionary meetings. He who has not sufficient interest in the work to desire to hear what is being done, will certainly not have sufficient interest to lead him to pray for the doing of it.

(b)—**Prayer for Missions must be Definite.**

What is true of study generally is true of missionary study. We should endeavour to know something about every mission, and everything about some mission. While we endeavour to keep ourselves informed as to the course of the movement over the whole field, we should have a special interest in some corner of the field. The Missionaries working there should be known to us by name. We should, if possible, make their personal acquaintance. We should count them our personal friends. Every scrap of information about them should be welcomed. The geography, the history, the ethnology of their field should be studied. Then our prayers will be definite, and growing in definiteness will grow in power.

(c)—**Prayer for Missions must be Intense.**

We must learn in this matter to labour in prayer. But what is implied in this? It implies our getting into sympathy with the mind of Christ. It implies that we look on the perishing multitudes with the eye of Christ, until His compassion fills our hearts. It means that there is borne in upon our hearts a new sense of their danger, a new sense of their awful loss in not knowing of the Christ. It means that by the Holy Ghost there is poured through our hearts such a tide of the love of Christ that we yearn over those lost souls as He yearned over the lost world. Then we kneel to pray, to labour, to wrestle, to agonise in prayer that labourers may be sent forth, full of faith and of the Holy Ghost to gather in those multitudes to the fold of Christ.

And it is thus "**by prayer and supplication, with thanksgiving,**" that our Heavenly Father has made it possible for all to be partakers in the privilege of bringing the Gospel to the heathen. Many of our readers may be unable, for various reasons, to go to the "Regions

Beyond." They may not have much to give either to Egypt or any other work, but everyone has the power and privilege of earnest prayer on behalf of those who have gone forth; and we would seek to enlist this prayer more directly and more earnestly for the land of Egypt at this time.

In the foregoing chapters we have endeavoured to present a general picture of the work at present being carried on in this ancient land. The national and political events of the last few months in Egypt have aroused so much interest in that country, that on every hand it is the subject of conversation and speculation. To the servant of God all points to the wonderful opportunity He is giving for the dissemination of the Gospel there. Hundreds of miles that have been sealed against the Gospel for years are now opened up, and the natives who have been kept down by the cruel yoke of the Mahdi, in their new found freedom, welcome the British soldier as the hero of their deliverance. Never before has such an opportunity presented itself of reaching this wild, yet brave people, with the glad tidings of free Salvation. It is anticipated that before long, under the protection of the British Government, the Missionaries of the Cross will reach still farther South, until they join hands with their brethren in the districts of Uganda and the Great Lakes.

Here is an open field worthy of the hearts and lives of every young man, or woman, who is willing to offer for the work. As the land is opening up, so may consecrated lives from the Home-land go in and " possess the country." Already the Church Missionary Society have Clergy, Doctors, Native Assistants, and, if opportunity arises, Trained Nurses ready to go to Khartoum as soon as the permission of those in authority is granted. Millions of people sitting in the bondage of a cruel and dark superstition, without a ray of light, or the knowledge of the true God, should surely awaken the cry, " Come over and help us!" May the Holy Spirit ring this message in the hearts of all those who are ready to obey the summons of their King. Here in the Home-land Christian workers overlap each other; out yonder is a vast region without any. Our nation supplies rulers, political officers, merchants, and men in all classes of business who go forth in secular callings for the mere sake of gain. The following from a daily paper on Trade in the Soudan indicates how keen the business man is for his own interests :—

"Trade is following the flag very quickly to Khartoum. We learn from the 'Commercial Traveller' that three well-known English, two German, two Belgian, and one French merchant are already well near to the front with a total of over 300 tons of merchandise. Nay, the advertising fiend has arrived there, one gentleman being commissioned to keep a smart look-out for every point favourable to the advertiser. Soaps and soups will soon flaunt their competitive blazons on the Mahdi's tomb."

Is it too much to expect that the splendid opportunity thus opening to the young consecrated lives of our land at this time will pass by without an adequate response? Can we not out of our abundance give to the help of those in need? Let us pray for Egypt as we have never done before, and pray definitely for every one we know there, and for every Missionary Association at work; and as we pray may the Holy Spirit reveal to each of us our individual responsibility in the matter, and while our country considers its honour at stake if there is no improvement in Government, shall not we as representatives of the King of Kings feel that we have left undone our duty if we have not responded to the opportunity of going forth to win dark Egypt for Jesus.

The existing Missionary Agencies will gladly give particulars as to the men and women who are wanted, and how their services can be best utilised. What is needed is that we may individually call upon our God, and open our hearts before Him, telling Him that we are willing to obey His summons, if He calls, that His promise may be fulfilled—"BLESSED BE EGYPT."

To help those wishing to apply, the following addresses are given:—

THE AMERICAN UNITED PRESBYTERIAN MISSION,
CAIRO, EGYPT.

THE CHURCH MISSIONARY SOCIETY,
SALISBURY SQUARE, LONDON, E.C.

THE NORTH AFRICA MISSION,
32, LINTON ROAD, BARKING, ESSEX.

The Prayer Union for Egypt

was formed in May, 1896, by a few friends who felt the intense need of the country, and who sought to hold up the hands of the Missionaries working there. Little effort was made to induce anyone to join, but the number of members gradually increased to one hundred and sixteen, and cards were also sent to America for friends who felt drawn to join in prayer with the English Christians for the land which had so long been laid to heart by them. Many of the Missionaries in the field joined the Union, and a few natives. A cycle of prayer was drawn up in order that each individual missionary and mission station belonging to each society might be remembered in continual intercession. Abundant cause for thanksgiving for answered prayer has been granted by our God who is more ready to hear than we to pray.

When the Egypt Mission Band was formed in 1897 it was felt that special prayer was needed for them, and that their circle of friends should be asked to unite with them in carrying on this new effort, which was only and utterly dependant on their faithful God. Upwards of three hundred personal friends of the little band of seven have joined together in the

Egypt Mission Band Prayer Circle.

The names of the secretaries of both Unions are given below, and they will gladly send cards of membership to any who would like to join them. Special reminders will be sent out from time to time with requests for prayer, and giving information of immediate and pressing causes for intercession. "By faith the walls of Jericho fell down."

Prayer Union for Egypt—
MISS A. VAN SOMMER,
CUFFNELLS, WIMBLEDON, SURREY.

EGYPT, 1898.

Special Needs for Prayer during this Year, together with the continual needs which we would bring to God.

1.—That the Gospel may be carried to the whole land of Egypt from Alexandria to Khartoum ; and that those already at work, and those preparing to go, may be trained and fitted by God both spiritually and in gaining a mastery of the language.

2.—For the English in Authority, that they may seek God's will, and that Christ's Name may be honoured, and His day kept holy : and that their power and influence may be fearlessly exerted for Him.

3.—For the Native Rulers and Officials, that they may come in contact with Christians, and may be convinced by their lives, of the truth of their Religion.

4.—For the University of Al-Azhar, that the 5,000 Moslem Students may lose their faith in Mohammed, and that doors may be kept open for telling them of Christ ; and that the Holy Ghost may work amongst them in conversions.

5.—For the Copts, that the Spirit of God may be poured out upon them, and that men of God may be raised up amongst themselves to preach words of life from Him.

6.—For work amongst young men in connection with the Y.M.C.A., and that this may be extended amongst young men of all nationalities.

7.—For work amongst girls in connection with the Y.W.C.A., and that this may be extended amongst girls of all nationalities.

8.—For the Sailors' and Soldiers' Institute, Alexandria, and for Rev. T. R. Lawrence and Mrs. Lawrence.

9.—Helouan. For the Church Missionary Society : Rev. F. F. Adeney (Secretary) and Mrs. Adeney. Cairo : Rev. J. C. B. Hollins and Mrs. Hollins, Mrs. Bywater, Miss J. B. Bywater, Miss H. Adeney, Miss M. J. Greer, Miss E. F. Waller. Old Cairo : Dr. F. J. Harpur and Mrs. Harpur, Dr. A. C. Hall and Mrs. Hall, Miss M. Cay, Miss E. A. Lawford, Miss F. M. Sells, Miss L. Crowther, and all Native Helpers.

10.—Cairo. The American Mission : The Rev. S. C. Ewing and Mrs. Ewing, Rev. W. Harvey, D.D., and Mrs. Harvey, Rev. Andrew Watson, D.D., and Mrs. Watson, Rev. John Giffen and Mrs. Giffen, Rev. J. Krudenier and Mrs. Krudenier, Rev. J. G. Hunt and Mrs. Hunt, Miss Anna Thompson, Miss Margaret Smith, Miss Ella Kyle, Miss Grace Brown.

11.—For Alexandria. The Scotch Church, and the Jewish Mission : Rev. W. Cowan and Mrs. Cowan, Rev. M. Taylor and Mrs. Taylor, Miss Kirkpatrick, Mrs. Gibb, Mrs. Robinson, Mr. Buchanan, Mr. Gordon, Mr. Kestin, Mr. Shimmins, and all Teachers and Assistants.

12.—For Alexandria. The American Mission: Rev. Thomas Finney and Mrs. Finney, Rev. Geo. A. Sowash and Mrs. Sowash, Miss Leonora McDowell, Miss Adele McMillan.

13.—For Alexandria. North Africa Mission: Mr. W. Summers and Mrs. Summers, Mr. W. Dickens and Mrs. Dickens, Mr. Hooper, Mr. and Mrs. Fairman, Mr. Kumm.

14.—The British and Foreign Bible Society: Rev. R. Weakley, and Rev. —— Cooper. And for the American Bible Society in Cairo. That God's blessing may rest on all portions of the Holy Scriptures throughout the country, and for all Christian Literature. That this work may be largely increased and greatly prospered.

15.—A Mission Band from Belfast and Glasgow: Mr. W. Bradley, Mr. J. Martin Cleaver, Mr. Frederick Cooney, Mr. John Gordon Logan, Mr. Edward Swan, Mr. George Swan, Mr. Elias H. Thompson.

16.—Mr. Stewart in his work among English Soldiers in Cairo. That God may raise up a Soldiers' Home in that City, and that Mrs. Todd Osborne may be prospered in her effort to establish one.

17.—For Mr. Peter Rudolph and his work among the poor Jews, Greeks, and others in Alexandria. For Signor Grisafi and his work among the Italians; and for the German Hospitals and Deaconesses, in both Cairo and Alexandria.

18.—For Monsúrah. American Mission: The Rev. J. P. White, M.D., and Mrs. White, Miss Minnehaha Finney.

19.—For Assioot. American Mission: Rev. J. R. Alexander, D.D., and Mrs. Alexander, Rev. E. M. Giffen and Mrs. Giffen, Rev. S. G. Hart and Mrs. Hart, Professor R. M'Clenahan and Mrs. M'Clenahan, Dr. L. M. Henry and Mrs. Henry, Miss Jessie Hogg, Miss Carrie Buchanan, Miss L. Teas, Miss Cora Dickey.

20.—For Benha. American Mission: Rev. C. Murch and Mrs. Murch.

21.—For Zagazig. American Mission: The Rev. K. W. Macfarland and Mrs. Macfarland.

22.—For Tanta. American Mission: Rev. J. Kelly Giffen and Mrs. Giffen, Dr. Anna Watson, Dr. Caroline Lawrence.

23.—For Luxor. American Mission: Rev. W. M. Nichol and Mrs. Nichol.

24.—For Semaloot. American Mission: Rev. W. H. Reed and Mrs. Reed.

25.—For Maghagha. American Mission: Rev. David Strang, D.D.

26.—For Damietta. American Mission, and all Native Helpers and Mission Schools throughout the Land.

27.—For Rosetta. The North Africa Mission: Miss Watson, Miss Van der Molen.

28.—Port Said. Mr. Locke, Mr Eoll, working among the Sailors.

29.—For Miss Rose Johnson and all other Workers whose names are unknown.

30.—For all secret believers in Christ, that they may have courage to confess Him.

31.—For our Prayer Union, that we may all continue in prayer, and that it shall be indeed the prayer of faith, which God loves to answer.

⁂ *Some of the above-mentioned are at home on furlough, but hope to return to Egypt.*

JOHN E. PIM, Hon. Sec.,
BONAVEN, ANTRIM ROAD, BELFAST.

"Ye also helping together by prayer for us."
—2 Cor. i. 11.

THAT *we may be kept " blameless and harmless, the sons of God without rebuke."*

THAT *we may be kept in living union with our Lord, and in unbroken unity with one another.*—JOHN xvii. 21.

THAT *our Master's will for us may be made plain from day to day, to the end*

THAT SOULS MAY BE WON FOR HIM.

WILLIAM BRADLEY.   T. ED. SWAN.
FREDK. G. COONEY.   GEORGE SWAN.
JOHN GORDON LOGAN. ELIAS H. THOMPSON.
J. MARTIN CLEAVER, *Hon. Sec.*,

Address—Beit-el-Hamd, Moharrem Bey,
Alexandria, Egypt.

"Thus saith the Lord, I will for this be enquired of .. to do it."—EZEK. xxxvi. 37.

———✱———

Home Friends who undertake Correspondence, and to be links of Communication:

REV. E. L. HAMILTON, Bath.
W. PENN-LEWIS, 48, Springfield Road, Leicester.
MISS LOGAN, 5, Granby Terrace, Glasgow, W.
A. W. VANCE, Chlorine, Belfast *(Hon. Treas.)*.
JOHN E. PIM *(Hon. Sec. Prayer Circle)*, Bonaven, Antrim Road, Belfast,

From whom Membership Cards can be obtained.

———

WM. STRAIN & SONS, PRINTERS, BELFAST.

www.ingramcontent.com/pod-product-compliance
Lightning Source LLC
Chambersburg PA
CBHW020155170426
43199CB00010B/1055